THE CONSCIO
GUID

Gender Identity

BUILD CONFIDENCE

A mindful approach to embracing your child's authentic self

PROMOTE ACCEPTANCE

STRENGTHEN YOUR RELATIONSHIP

Darlene Tando, LCSW

Adams Media
New York London Toronto Sydney New Delhi

Adams Media
An Imprint of Simon & Schuster, Inc.
100 Technology Center Drive
Stoughton, Massachusetts 02072

For information about special discounts for bulk purchases, please contact Simon & Schuster Special Sales at 1-866-506-1949 or *business@simonandschuster.com*.

The Simon & Schuster Speakers Bureau can bring authors to your live event. For more information or to book an event contact the Simon & Schuster Speakers Bureau at 1-866-248-3049 or visit our website at *www.simonspeakers.com*.

Manufactured in the United States of America

2 2021

ISBN 10: 1-4405-9630-1
ISBN 13: 978-1-4405-9630-8 (ebook)

DEDICATION

This book is dedicated to my two amazing children. You light up my life every day! Thank you for sharing me as I try to make the world a better place.

This book is also dedicated to all "my" other children; thank you for letting me be a part of your life. You will always have a special place in my heart.

Contents

Acknowledgments

I would like to express my deepest appreciation to those who have supported me in writing this book, both personally and professionally. Thank you to my wonderful friends and family for believing in me as I tried to "do it all." Special thanks goes to Ashley, Kim, Kate, Bonnie, Julie, John, Nora, Rich, Tami, and my parents Ted and Linda for supporting me with words of encouragement and helping me out with my kids to allow time to write. I'd also like to thank Evan for encouraging me to start and write my gender blog, which led me to this book.

I'd like to extend my sincerest gratitude to my clients and colleagues who carried the excitement about this book for me as I hunkered down to write. Thank you to my sounding boards: Jo, Aydin, a.t., Will, Asaf, and Julie; your input was invaluable. I also wish to acknowledge *all* of my clients who inspire and teach me every day. Thank you to the families I work with for trusting me with your children and allowing me to walk this journey with you. It is nothing short of an honor to bear witness to your pain, triumphs, and unconditional love. Thank you to my adult gender expansive and transgender clients; allowing me glimpses into your hearts and your childhoods reinforces why it is so important for gender expansive children of today to be affirmed and celebrated.

Lastly, but most importantly, I'd like to thank KD. Thank you for trusting me and opening the door to this world for me. I'm eternally grateful.

Introduction

There may be a number of reasons why you chose to read this book. Perhaps you are raising a gender-expansive child (a child who expands beyond what is expected for their assigned gender at birth, either in expression or identity) and want to be sure you are doing it in the most conscious way possible. Perhaps you are already a conscious parent who has recently realized you are raising a gender-expansive child and want to learn more about the topic. Maybe you have seen a persistent and consistent gender expansiveness in your child, and you want to make sure you are responding in a way that is best for their development.

For those of you further along in the journey, some of this book will feel like review. For those of you new to the gender-expansive journey, welcome! It can seem overwhelming at first, but please remember you don't have to know everything about gender and all its intricacies right from the start.

If you have just started noticing or realizing your child's gender expansiveness, you may feel a sense of urgency and feel like you can't read this book fast enough. Give yourself permission to slow down. There is likely no emergency. Give yourself time and space to breathe and think so you can ground yourself in such a way that will help you feel more prepared to walk this journey with your child.

One core concept to get you started is that an accepting, affirmative approach is best for your gender-expansive child. In your behaviors, decisions, and statements to your child, communicate this: "Any way you are is okay."

Another core concept from which to operate is that you do not have to have all the answers. Your child likely has many answers waiting to be revealed. Ask many questions! If your child communicates to you (either verbally or nonverbally) that they are feeling like they have a gender identity other than their assigned gender at birth, ask questions. Explore. Over time, your child's authentic self will become more clear.

When you first notice your child's gender expansiveness, or recognize a gender identity that is different from what you expected, you will likely need to quiet the interference in your head. You may begin to worry in the form of "what ifs." You may start to imagine negative input from outside sources, and you might begin thinking about how you will explain your child's gender expression or gender identity to others. You may start to get caught up in your own expectations and make projections onto your child, getting swept away by resulting emotions. When this happens, pause for a moment. Come back to the right now, the place and time where you are with your child. Quiet the interfering voices and know that the most important voice is that of your child's. The only way you will hear it is if you are connected to your child and conscious, mindful of the present moment. Remind yourself this is about your child and their happiness, and that they are your guide on this journey.

If your child is expansive in their gender expression, try to consistently come from an affirming place. Allow your child to express themselves in a way that seems to come from their most authentic place. Do not try to control it or warn about potential reactions of others. If your child verbally discloses their alternate gender identity, ask questions. You don't have to give answers. If you are feeling particularly stumped by a question, turn it around. "I don't know, what do *you* think?" Other exploratory, open-ended questions include:

O What makes you think that?

O How do you know that?

O What is your heart telling you?

O What feels right?

O What is the little voice inside telling you?

○ How did you figure that out?

○ Why do you think it's like that?

○ How do you feel about that?

The process of your child revealing exactly what they need and who they are, as well as you coming to understand all the many aspects of your child's identity, is an evolutionary process. Take your time. Enjoy your child along the way.

 **CHAPTER 1**

Conscious Parenting

Being a conscious parent is all about building strong, sustainable bonds with your child through mindful living and awareness. Traditional power-based parenting techniques that promote compliance and obedience can disconnect you from your child. Conscious parenting, on the other hand, helps you develop a positive emotional connection with your child. You acknowledge your child's unique self and attempt to empathize with their way of viewing the world. Through empathetic understanding and compassion you create a safe environment where your child feels their ideas and concerns are truly being heard. This approach benefits all children, especially children who are gender-expansive or transgender. These children need you to be able to stay open and stay with them on their gender journey, through all the twists and turns. Additionally, because gender-expansive journeys can have some challenges, staying in a place of acceptance for yourself and your child without judgment is crucial for the well-being of both of you.

The Benefits of Conscious Parenting

Conscious parenting isn't a set of rules or regulations that you must follow, rather it is a system of beliefs. Conscious parents engage and connect with their child, using mindful and positive discipline rather than punishment. They try to be present when they're spending time with their children, minimizing distractions like TV and social media. Conscious parents respect their child and accept them as they are. This is crucial when raising a gender-expansive child.

You must build an emotional connection with your child so that you can understand the underlying reasons for their behavior. This is the most important part of conscious parenting. Conscious parents build a secure attachment with their child that helps them make grounded, timely responses to their child's needs. When you are in tune with your gender-expansive child you will be more responsive to them, and your responses will be more appropriate.

Conscious parenting is about listening with full attention, and embracing a nonjudgmental acceptance of yourself and your child. As you engage in the act of becoming a more conscious parent, you will discover a heightened sense of emotional awareness of yourself and your child, a clearer self-regulation in the parenting relationship, and a greater compassion for yourself and your child.

Conscious parenting brings with it a number of benefits including improved communication, stronger relationships, and the feeling of greater happiness and satisfaction in life. Some of these benefits appear more immediately, while others take some time to emerge. Conscious parenting and mindfulness produce benefits when you make them a part of your daily life. With practice, conscious parenting becomes an integral part of who and how you are in the world, and will in turn become a central part of who your child is as well.

Adopting the conscious parent philosophy can relieve your stress and improve your child's self-image. The strong bond built between you and your child, along with your own calm, respectful attitude, help them to develop positive behavior patterns. Modeling acceptance and affirmation regarding your child's gender identity will help them do the same. Conscious parenting is all about a child's self-determination, and what better way to put this into action than by respecting your child as the "expert" on their own gender identity? When you focus on the well-being of your child, and allow them to grow in the most natural way possible, you give them much more opportunity to live a life that is true to their authentic self.

SELF-AWARENESS AND SELF-CONTROL

One of the first benefits of conscious parenting that you (and your child) will see is a heightened awareness of yourself and your inner life, including your emotions, thoughts, and feelings. As you become more aware of these various forces moving within you, you can begin to watch them rise without being at their mercy. For example, when you are aware that you are becoming angry, you can choose whether or not to act from that anger. Instead of acting out, you can attend to that feeling of anger directly. You will start to notice the things that tend to set you off, your triggers, and you will begin to be able to anticipate your emotions before they have a hold on you. When you find yourself in a stressful situation with your child, rather than reacting with anger or sarcasm, conscious parenting reminds you to instead take a step back, reflect, and look for a peaceful solution—one that honors your child's individuality and motivations.

Mindfulness is the practice of being attentive in any given moment, and noticing what is taking place both inside and outside of you without judgment. It is the practice of purposefully seeing your thoughts, emotions, experiences, and surroundings as they arise. Simply put, mindfulness is the act of paying attention.

As you become more skilled at noticing your thoughts and feelings that arise, you will begin to notice them more quickly, maybe even before they start to affect your actions. This awareness is itself a powerful tool. It opens up the possibility to say, "I'm pretty mad right now . . ." as opposed to yelling. Self-awareness can do exactly the same thing for your child, helping them to learn to communicate their feelings rather than just to react from that place of emotion. As with most things, children learn this best when seeing it modeled by the adults in their lives.

Often, you may notice that your emotions carry with them a sense of urgency. As you feel the rising impulse to do something, mindfulness helps you see the forces driving that sense of "I need to do something." For example, watching a three-year-old put on their own shoes can produce strong feelings and impatient thoughts. Your mind might be buzzing with impatience, and you might think, "I need to put their shoes on for them because they're taking forever." When you notice this thought, instead of immediately acting on it be self-aware to allow for some room to check in with yourself and act intentionally. In that particular moment, you may be able to remind yourself of the importance of your child learning self-efficacy and independence. Ultimately, this lesson is more important than the ten to twenty seconds you may save by helping them with their shoes. This practice of noticing creates a certain amount of mental space in which you can deal with a given thought, or feeling itself, rather than being moved to act on it.

WELL-BEING

Conscious parents understand that all they do and say over the course of each day matters. It is a sense of the now, of being in the present moment without regard or worry for the past or future. When you become more mindful, you may find that you become more accepting of the things in life that you can't change. As a result, you will experience less stress. The net result is greater satisfaction and enjoyment of what each day has to offer. This sense of well-being offers a satisfaction and contentment in knowing that we are who we are intended to be, doing precisely what we are designed for in the moment. As you prepare to walk with your child on this gender journey, staying in the moment will be hugely beneficial to both of you.

As human beings, we each possess the tools for contributing something of value. Assess your gifts and talents—those personality traits and skills that make you unique—and determine how to employ them to enhance your parenting. If you take a full accounting of yourself—good, bad, and indifferent—and own the sum total of your individual experience, you are taking the first step toward conscious parenting.

EMPATHY

The awareness you gain as a conscious parent redefines your perception of yourself and your compassionate understanding of your child. This serves a practical purpose: When you understand how your child experiences the world and how they learn, you can communicate in ways that really reach them. This largely happens through modeling, or teaching through example. Doing so allows you to pass on the values and lessons that are important to you, regardless of your beliefs.

Allowing yourself to let your child show you exactly who they are in regard to gender is the only way you will be able to support them in the ways they need it most.

ACCEPTANCE AND VALIDATION

Your child relies upon you to provide a solid foundation of self-esteem. Equipped with a strong sense of self-worth, your child will be better prepared to enter into a life that will likely present many challenges (as all lives do). Much of your time and energy will be expended in raising, counseling, and disciplining your child in ways that they will understand. It is important to try to equalize those occasions by reinforcing your love and appreciation of their gifts and talents.

Giving Your Child Full Attention

All too often people multitask their way through the day. This is a coping mechanism you have probably developed to juggle the many projects, tasks, errands, and obligations that you are responsible for. Although multitasking is a common approach to managing multiple things, it splits your attention in ways that distract your mind and actually lessens the quality of your attention. In reality, heavy multitasking causes your work and social interactions to suffer because of how it divides your focus.

To avoid this becoming an issue between you and your child (and to make sure you're modeling the kind of focus and engagement you want your child to use as well), make sure to practice engaged listening when you are at home with your family. This means setting aside other distractions, making eye contact, and giving the speaker (in this case, your child) your full attention.

Multitasking is neurologically impossible. When you try to multitask, what you actually end up doing is rapidly switching between tasks. Each time you do so, you lose efficiency and concentration. Instead, do one thing at a time so you can do it with your whole brain, and then move on to the next task.

Once you have stopped what you were doing and are looking at your child, check in with yourself. Is your mind focused on what they are saying, or is it still planning, scheduling, remembering, projecting, or worrying? It is very easy to only half-listen, and this can be especially true when it comes to listening to children. The stories your child tells are not always relevant or very interesting to your adult life. The idea behind active listening is not that you suddenly care about what everyone else brought to school for Show and Tell today. Rather, it's about demonstrating that you care about your child when they want to tell you the funny, strange, or interesting things that they experienced during the day. The important part of this interaction is that your child wants to share their joy, curiosity, and interests with you. They want to interact with you and share parts of themselves and their life with you, and this is one of the ways they can do that. Don't miss out on this gift, even if the subject itself bores you. You'll be surprised by the interest you may develop in these things as you listen to your child. When a person you love cares about something, it becomes easier to see that "something" through their eyes and come to appreciate it all the more. Additionally, when your child feels you listen about minor details of their life, they will trust you more when it comes to significant details.

Understanding Behavior

It can be developmentally appropriate for children to express emotions through behavior. Additionally, because young children have yet to develop complex language skills to describe their gender and/or how their gender expansiveness is affecting them, they may communicate this more with behaviors. It's important that you (as their liaison to the world) interpret their behaviors in order to understand the underlying emotions and the larger communication they are trying to express. All external behaviors are a reflection of what your child's inner emotional world looks like.

Attempt to view your child's behavior as a message; it is a message about what your child is currently experiencing. If your child is exhibiting undesirable behaviors, they are probably not trying to intentionally upset you. Rather, they are likely experiencing some undesirable emotions! Behaviors that are undesirable on behalf of your child can provoke your unconscious mind to take over. If that happens, you will be unable to objectively view the behaviors as information. A conscious parent will try to get in touch with the motivation behind a child's behavior. Do your best to avoid responding to your child in anger. When you react with anger, you miss the opportunity to find out what has prompted the upset in your child. If you respond to your child's behaviors with compassion and connection, you will be better able to get to the root of the feelings. Once you can better understand what is motivating the behavior, you can partner with your child in finding more appropriate ways of releasing those emotions.

Negative behaviors one may see in a gender-expansive child will likely have to do more with how they are censored and limited in their preferences than anything else. You may see your child battling intensely in resistance to certain types of clothing. You may witness your child withdrawing from social interactions or public outings if they do not feel they can express themselves authentically. You may see shyness in social interactions as they monitor their behavior for their peers. Resentment, shame, and anxiety can develop if a child's gender identity or preferences are not affirmed and accepted, resulting in anger outbursts or meltdowns. Sometimes, feelings about gender identity can also come out in such misbehaviors. Those individuals in charge of a child's emotional care may be the ones who bear the brunt of these emotional outbursts.

Understanding the feelings and motivations behind the behavior does not mean you allow unsafe or inappropriate behavior, nor does it mean that you don't set limits. Using empathy, tolerance, and the validation of needs will make your influence stronger with your child, all while assuring the child that they are loved. When a child is secure in these foundational relationship aspects, they are more likely to listen and follow the limits you establish. Additionally, modeling self-regulation and mindful practices will allow your child to work on these skills as well.

> If you give up trying to control your child's gender expression and/or communication of gender identity, and focus instead on unconditional love and acceptance, you give your child space to truly live authentically. It is only then that you will see your child for who they genuinely are, and allow your child's inner happiness and gifts to reach their full capacity.

Important Points to Consider

Conscious parenting is a deliberate, loving, and carefully applied way of interacting with your child that allows both of you to be honored for the unique individuals you are. This style of parenting capitalizes on strengths. Minimizing outside influences and focusing on what makes your child calm, confident, and truly content is an important part of applying conscious parenting to a gender-expansive and/or transgender child. Another key concept of staying in tune with your child is to monitor their mood and watch for signs of distress. Specifically:

- When does my child seem happiest?
- What is my child's greatest source of distress?
- Am I trying to control my child's gender/gender expression, or am I allowing my child to be free to show me who they are?
- When has my child appeared the most calm, confident, and content? Were they at the helm of their gender ship at the time?

Relinquishing control of your child's gender identity or expression not only positively affects your child but also releases you from the responsibility of trying to control something that does not need controlling. All family members can then relax into a mode just "being" exactly as they are.

Gender 101

Gender is all around you. From the time you are born, gender is present. In fact, your "gender" is usually the first thing people talk about when you enter the world. For some people, experiencing gender can be relatively easy, given that they do not have obstacles for understanding or having others understand their true gender. For others, gender can be complicated. This is mainly because of having to navigate a society that places so much emphasis on gender, and yet misunderstands gender at the same time.

Gender versus Sex

Contrary to popular belief, one's "gender" does not mean the same thing as one's "sex." The two words mean different things. However, because the majority of individuals feel their gender "matches" their sex, these terms are mistakenly thought to be interchangeable. The term for someone who considers their authentic gender identity to be congruent with their sex at birth is *cisgender*. The term for someone who feels their authentic gender identity to be incongruent with their sex at birth is *transgender*.

The term *gender* is in reference to what a person feels like internally, or their sense of self in regard to gender. This can be male, female, a blend of both, variable depending on time and circumstance, or neither male nor female. If one identifies as having a male gender, the individual is most likely going to be comfortable being called (what society considers) a male name, may use he/him/his pronouns, and will likely want to be read as male in society. If one has a female gender identity, she is most likely going to want to be referred to by a female name, the pronouns she/her/hers, and will probably want to be read as female in society. For those who feel more gender-fluid, how they feel gender-wise can fluctuate. This may cause them to want to use different pronouns at different times, depending on how they feel. For those who do not identify as either male or female, or perhaps a blend of both, they may opt for gender-neutral pronouns.

The term *sex* refers to genitals and sex organs; male or female genitals/sex organs make one anatomically male or female. Those with female genitalia and sex organs are assigned female at birth. Similarly, those with male genitalia and sex organs are assigned male at birth. If one has ambiguous genitalia or a blend of both male and female sex organs, chromosomes, and/or hormones, that condition is called *intersex*. Please refer to Appendix C to see how sex and gender are different.

ASSIGNED GENDER

Expectant parents are often eager to find out the "gender" of their unborn baby, either by way of ultrasound when the baby is still in the womb, or at birth when the genitals are revealed. This is actually a misnomer, because only the genitals of the baby are being revealed, not the gender. Gender will not be able to be communicated until the individual can speak and communicate their gender. One's gender identity comes from one's internal sense of self and may or may not align with the sex that one is assigned at birth.

Consider this: When you check out at the grocery store, do you want someone to say "Thank you, Ma'am" or "Thank you, Sir"? This acknowledgment is a way of simplifying gender as it relates to an everyday experience. For most people, it would feel uncomfortable to be addressed as something that wasn't consistent with their authentic gender identity. In everyday experiences like these, sex organs don't matter, but minds certainly do.

When a baby is born the parents hear "It's a boy!" or "It's a girl!"; that is a statement of the baby's sex. It would be more accurate to say "Your baby has a penis!" or "Your baby has a vagina!" When the sex of the baby is automatically assumed to represent the gender, this is called "assigned gender at birth." Babies with vaginas are "assigned" female and babies with penises are "assigned" male. However, it's worth repeating that one's true gender is revealed much later, when the individual becomes old enough or aware enough to express their authentic gender identity. The distinction between gender and sex is an important one. The more society can understand that these two concepts are different, the better life will be for transgender individuals.

Being transgender is having the authentic gender identity of something other than the sex (and therefore "assigned gender") at birth. Since gender is an internal experience (that then needs to be externally communicated in order to be understood), gender identity typically comes down to how we feel and how we think. In order to communicate this concept to children, this can be symbolized with "hearts" and "brains."

Of course, this is only one part in the exploration of gender identity with children, but the simplicity of terms makes it easier for children to understand and communicate. Children tend to seem relieved when they learn who they are in their heart and brain is their valid, authentic gender.

> A child (assigned female at birth) may feel she has the heart and brain of a girl, therefore making her a cisgender girl. A child (assigned female at birth) may feel like they have the heart and brain of a boy, possibly indicating they may be transgender. They may disclose they feel like a blend of genders or no gender, which may suggest an identity that does not fall within the gender binary.

Gender Identity versus Sexual Orientation

Gender identity refers to what your authentic gender is, who you are, and how you want others to see you. What gender you identify with is going to impact many areas of your life, if not all. It will affect how you are seen in society, how others respond to you, how you are addressed, expectations for your behavior, where you go to the bathroom, your role in your family, your romantic relationships, and much more.

Sexual orientation refers to who you are attracted to, who you would like to receive romantic attention/affection from, and who you would like to be sexually intimate with. Sexual orientation not only refers to the sex (anatomy) one is attracted to, but also the gender. Certainly, anatomy plays a role in sexual relationships, but the gender of the individual is likely what initiates the attraction in the first place. Additionally, gender can be more of a factor in dating and relationships than one's anatomy.

Do children have a gender identity? Yes, usually children have a clear understanding of being either a boy or a girl. Some children feel like they are both a boy and a girl, or neither a boy or a girl. These children may not seem as "sure" about their gender identity, and this is largely because society has not allowed much room for understanding an individual who does not land on the gender binary. Children are not raised to hear "sometimes people feel like both a boy and a girl, and sometimes they feel like neither," so they don't exactly know how to express it themselves. They may try to conform to one end of the binary because they know it is expected of them, even if it does not feel quite right. If you can't remember thinking about your gender as a child, it's likely because your authentic gender identity matched with your assigned sex or assigned gender at birth.

Do children have a sexual orientation? Yes, but usually not one that is conscious or that expresses itself at a young age. Children are not sexual beings. However, at what age do you remember "liking" or having crushes on other people? Developmentally, this usually happens in elementary school. Proper "sexual" attraction may not be present, but whispering about, sending notes to, and giggling in the presence of one's crush usually is. Therefore, it is at this age when most children realize which gender(s) they are attracted to, but this attraction won't become a sexual idea for some time.

EVERYDAY LIFE

Ultimately, who you are sexually attracted to is just one element of who you are and how you relate to others on a day-to-day basis. To whom you are attracted doesn't matter when you are checking out at the grocery store. Gender identity, however, is a more pervasive issue and one that affects an individual even more regularly than sexual orientation.

> Depending on your cultural environment, who you are sexually intimate with or attracted to may not impact you on a daily basis or how you interact with society. Additionally, you may not be involved with *anyone* sexually or romantically, but your gender and how it impacts you and how you relate to the world is largely unavoidable.

WHAT DEFINES US?

Sometimes so much emphasis is placed on sexual orientation it can seem as though it defines a person. Sexual orientation does not define a person as much as gender identity. For example, some people may be curious as to why a transgender man goes to such lengths to transition, when it may have just been "easier" to live life "as a lesbian." Putting aside assumptions about sexual orientation for a moment, while transition can be difficult, there is nothing easy about living a life that feels incongruent to who you authentically are.

Staying socially/physically female and identifying "as a lesbian" would allow this transgender man to continue to date women if so preferred, but all other areas of life would be more difficult. For example, think of the traditional names "Mom" and "Dad," terms that are typically used for female- and male-identified parents. If this transgender man were to live his life "as a lesbian" and had children, his name might be "Mom" or a version thereof. This simply doesn't fit with his gender identity and would likely sound as strange to him as it would to any assigned male who is a father. Another example would be this same person (continuing to present as female) taking a female partner out to dinner and the server saying, "Hello, ladies." Cringing inside every time they hear the reference to themselves as female if it does not feel authentic is most certainly not the "easier" way to go.

As for sexual orientation, living "as a lesbian" in reference to a transgender man is actually a misguided idea. A transgender man is not, and never has been, a lesbian. Yes, many transgender individuals come out as gay prior to understanding their gender identity or coming out as transgender. Because being gay is presently more accepted, understood, and talked about than being transgender, this may be the only way a transgender individual knows how to identify at first. If an assigned female is attracted to women, they may assume they are a lesbian and may come out as such, before realizing they actually identify as male. Oftentimes one's gender identity is understood later, which then invalidates a previously thought sexual orientation.

SEPARATE YET CONNECTED

The fact that gender identity and sexual orientation are two separate entities is precisely why someone can be transgender *and* gay. For example, an assigned male who has the brain gender identity of a female may transition to a woman and also be attracted to women, thereby making her a lesbian.

While these two concepts are different, they are not entirely separate. Gender identity and sexual orientation affect one another in dating/relationships. Sexual/romantic interactions are not only about who you are attracted to but are also about how you want your sexual/romantic partner to treat and perceive you. A transgender woman will likely want to be treated sexually as a woman (her gender identity), whether she is choosing to be sexual with a man or a woman (reflecting her sexual orientation). Additionally, one's gender identity must be factored in to understand one's sexual orientation. See Appendix C to visualize how gender, gender expression, and sexual orientation are each on their own spectrum.

Gender Expression

Gender expression refers to how a person may communicate gender, express gender, or perform gender. The ways of expressing gender are on a spectrum and are practically limitless. On the spectrum, gender expression can be feminine, masculine, androgynous, or an intricate blend of feminine and masculine. One's gender expression may be in line with one's gender identity or it may not; it may be in line with one's assigned gender at birth or it may not. One's gender expression may be relatively static, not changing much over time, or it may be dynamic, evolving and changing as time goes on. If one is gender-fluid in their gender expression, this can mean moving back and forth from masculine to feminine (see Appendix C). This may be reflective of a fluid gender identity (moving back and forth between genders), or it may not. Gender identity can remain static even when one's gender expression does not.

For example:

○ An individual may be male (gender identity) and present as androgynous (gender expression).

○ An individual may feel like a blend of both male and female (gender identity) and may present as masculine (gender expression).

○ An individual may identify as a woman (gender identity) and have a gender-fluid presentation, ranging from feminine to masculine depending on the day (gender expression).

○ An individual may identify as a man (gender identity) and present as feminine (gender expression).

To conform means to behave according to socially acceptable conventions or standards. The term *gender nonconforming* is typically used to describe someone who does not express gender in line with how society expects them to express it, based on either their assigned sex or gender identity. A gender nonconforming individual does not subscribe to society's gender "rules" about what colors/way of dress/interests are for differently gendered individuals. It is in this way that gender is a social construct, and it is influenced by time, culture, and environment.

We All Have a Gender Identity

Is gender pathological? No. Gender just is. It has neither good nor bad qualities. Gender is simply one's inner sense of being male, female, both, or neither, on the continuum between male and female, or beyond the spectrum of male/female. Gender in and of itself does not usually cause distress. Distress can come from feeling like your exterior presentation does not match your authentic gender identity, and distress can come from society not understanding your gender. We all have a gender identity even if that gender identity means not identifying with a gender at all. As a conscious parent, you will want to give space to your child to allow them to express their true gender identity, while remaining aware of how your own experience of gender, or expectations of gender, may impact your ability to do so. Simply knowing that everyone has their own gender identity is important, which will remind you that your child's gender identity is uniquely theirs, as is yours.

Most people are pretty certain of their gender identity. Cisgender and transgender people alike, most are pretty certain. What confounds things is that only transgender people have to navigate through having an authentic gender identity that differs from their birth sex. These individuals have to first understand their identity and then explain this to others. They receive confusing messages from society about their assigned gender at birth, and what is expected of them. This can interfere with their ability to assert their true gender or even understand it themselves. Still, most are fairly certain of their gender identity. Oftentimes, knowing one's gender identity is the "easy" part. Pursuing a life to align one's gender presentation and/or acknowledgment by others with one's authentic gender identity can be more challenging.

Every person is the expert on their own gender identity. Trust what they say to be true for them, even if you can't relate to it or haven't heard of it before. Operate from the standpoint that you are there to honor and respect their gender, not to decide what it is or what you are comfortable with. This includes honoring the name and pronouns they use to reflect their gender identity. The only way to have a relationship with someone is to honor them for who they truly are and allow them to be authentic in your presence.

NONBINARY IDENTITIES

The term *gender identity* does not mean just boy or girl, man or woman. Society tends to operate as though there are only two genders, male and female. In reality, male and female are but two genders that a person can be. Thinking of gender as being male *or* female is a binary way of looking at gender. Those individuals who do not identify as male or female have what are called nonbinary identities. Gender is not just two neat boxes that encompass all people. A person can feel male, female, a blend of both, in between both, or neither of these two. Some people feel "closer" to being male or being female but do not feel all male or female. Terms some individuals choose to use to describe their nonbinary identities are *genderqueer*, *neutrois*, or simply *nonbinary*.

All gender identities are individual and valid. Being transgender or having a nonbinary gender identity is just a variation of the human condition.

INCREASING AWARENESS

There seems to be an increasing number of individuals who are open about being genderqueer, agender, or otherwise beyond the gender binary and who are opting to use pronouns other than "he/him/his" or "she/her/hers." The most common of these are "they/them/theirs" or "ze/hir/hirs." But there is also a plethora of other options that can help an individual to try to best capture or reflect the way they feel gender-wise.

Because of this recent surge in terminology, naysayers may feel it is a phenomenom that is trendy, temporary, or is influenced by others who feel this way/peers/social media. In reality, people have been identifying as nonbinary for centuries. The burgeoning visibility of individuals who do not feel "on the binary" is likely tied to heightened awareness about this issue, which opens individuals up to what this aspect of the human experience can actually entail. The topic of gender has been visible recently, largely because of the Internet and mainstream media covering gender-expansive and transgender individuals. It's likely true that others who share about identifying this way in the media and the Internet play a role in this, as nowadays people tend to get much of their information from these mediums. However, if these mediums are giving people more information about what exists on the gender spectrum/continuum, this is a good thing.

Consider if you were raised to believe there were only two colors: black and white. Your whole life, you could see the rainbow of colors out there, but you didn't say anything for fear of being chastised or made to feel like you were making them up. Then one day, you find out about the rainbow and all the colors therein, and that plenty of other people can see them, too. You finally say "Yes, I've seen these colors my whole life. I just didn't know I could say there were colors outside of black and white."

Until gender is taught/discussed in less binary and more inclusive terms, children who feel outside of the gender binary will likely get information about experiences they can relate to from other sources.

SPECTRUMS

The Center for Gender Sanity created a "Diagram of Sex and Gender" that delineates the spectrums of assigned sex/gender identity/gender expression/sexual orientation. (You can find an updated/modified version in Appendix C.) This diagram is a tool that can be used to help someone understand the basics. One limitation of these spectrums is that they are very linear and very binary. "Male" and "Female" are at the ends of the gender identity spectrum, with genderqueer/agender in the middle. These concepts may be better exhibited by a more fluid and continuous structure, with the middle ground being the culmination of points rather than two ends of a binary. (See Appendix B for just a sampling of how the inter-play of these concepts can be expressed graphically.)

Gender Expansiveness

The term *gender-expansive* describes someone who identifies or expresses themselves outside of what is typically expected for assigned gender at birth. All transgender children are gender-expansive, but not all gender-expansive children are transgender.

A child may not express themselves, perform their gender, or feel in a way that is expected for a person of their assigned gender. Most of this is defined by social constructs, but some of it is indicative of differences in the way one's brain functions as it relates to gender. There is some basis to gender stereotypes, in that many people of a particular gender may be drawn to specific interests. The important thing is to not become so entrenched in these expectations that a child who does not fit the mold feels inadequate, or hides their authentic interests in order to fit in with mainstream society.

There have been many ways to describe gender expansiveness. A very common term is "gender nonconforming." As previously discussed, this concept is understood in relation to society and how an individual "conforms" (or not) to society's expectations. Gender "expansive" more broadly addresses being beyond what society expects for a gender, but perhaps also beyond what is typical for those of a certain gender. Other terms used for gender-expansive children include but are not limited to: gender-diverse, gender-variant, and gender-creative.

Does gender exist in a vacuum? If there were no societal expectations of gender molding/influencing/judging children, would their gender develop on one specific trajectory? One's brain gender identity typically "wires" us to prefer certain things, but not always. It's the "not always" that results in expansive gender expression. This is why introducing a more gender-neutral way of raising children is positive; while "most" children will subscribe to one set of behaviors and interests, for gender-expansive individuals it's the way we respond to the "not always" that is crucial.

If you consider how the color pink has been so strongly associated with "girls" and how blue typically represents "boys," then it should be clear to see how binary our society is. Most people assume everyone falls into one of those categories: boy or girl. In reality, "boy/girl," "pink/blue" doesn't even get close to covering the many facets of gender. Additionally, gender has traditionally been seen as a static characteristic. While for some folks it is, for some it is not. It is possible for gender to evolve over time or be transient.

GENDER TRANSITION

Transition, in general terms, is the process of changing oneself in order to be seen as one's authentic gender identity. Gender identity is who one is, and transition is something one does. One does not "become" transgender. One is born transgender. What one eventually does with that gender identity is an entirely different issue, and is different for every individual.

Understanding, knowing, discovering, and realizing one's gender identity is a unique process for everyone. Some people understand what gender they are from the very start, never think about it, and never have to worry about it their entire lives. These people are usually those whose assigned sex match their authentic gender (cisgender). For transgender individuals, coming to understand their personal gender can vary widely. Some have an immediate sense of identifying as another gender. Depending on temperament, family influence, and other factors, that awareness can cause very different levels of distress in the individual. Some are vocal about it. Some guard it like a secret. Some don't really know exactly what's going on, but they have a sense there is something they are not quite comfortable with. Some individuals don't realize their gender doesn't match their assigned sex until they are much older, but when they do, a lot of pieces fall into place.

Important Points to Consider

So much of understanding your gender-expansive child's authentic self has to do with understanding not only gender but also how your child's unique temperament and life circumstances all interact to form their unique gender expression and/or identity.

- Gender is an internal experience of how one conceptualizes oneself in relation to the male/female spectrum, and everything in between. Sex is an external/physical presentation, which may or may not align with one's brain gender identity.

- Gender identity is how one feels about themselves, their psychological sense of self as it relates to gender.

- Everything, including gender, gender expression, and sexual orientation, is on a spectrum or a continuum. All the spectrums interact to weave a beautiful pattern that is unique to each of us.

- Gender expression is how one communicates or performs gender. Gender expansiveness is a liberated, unique way of expressing gender without the confines of societal constructs or preconceived notions of gender.

- Being more informed about the various spectrums and the multiplicities of possibilities regarding what forms one's self, you will be able to be more in tune with what your child is displaying as it relates to these various elements.

 **CHAPTER 3**

Connecting to Your Child

Staying connected to your child is the best way to ensure this gender journey is authentic and focused on the needs of your child. In fact, being connected to your child benefits almost *all* aspects of the parent/child dynamic. When you are connected to your child, you know that your child's external behavior and presentation is a reflection of their internal landscape, and it helps you respond accordingly. A loving, supportive relationship with your child facilitates a realness that not only allows you to understand your child's gender but also affords you the peace to trust yourself.

Listen Carefully

Conscious parenting is about listening and responding to your child in a way that honors their individuality. Being connected with your child helps you recognize that they are a separate, conscious being with real feelings, motivations, and needs worthy of attention and respect. The only way to truly understand your child's needs and support them is to genuinely listen to what they have to tell you. Sometimes, this listening is with your ears when they are using words, and sometimes you must listen with your heart when they are not.

MINIMIZE DISTRACTIONS

In this age of technology and overbooked schedules, being present without distraction can be quite challenging. Parents often find themselves attuning to their child *and* something else at the same time. While it may seem necessary, this is the very definition of not being present.

If you are consistently distracted when you are with your child, you have the potential to miss a lot when it comes to what they are trying to tell you. While it may be impossible to give your child 100 percent attention every time they talk to you, it is essential they have the chance to talk to you with your full, undivided attention at least once every day.

Ask yourself what space you need to get into in order to listen fully to your child. What distractions need to be set aside? How do you communicate that you understand what your child is telling you is important? For some parents this may mean setting aside their work. For other parents it may mean turning off the television, phone, or other distracting electronics. Responding to an electronic alert while your child is talking to you sends the message they are not top priority.

It is only when these other distractions have been put to rest that your child will feel the open invitation to share authentically with you. Even if what your child is telling you does not seem momentous, it is important enough to them that they have chosen to share it with you. When you listen actively on a regular basis, they learn you are open and receptive. This creates a foundation that will promote ongoing communication of their internal experience, including gender. This is especially important as they get older, as inhibitions and developmental boundaries come into play.

Particularly with gender, your child may need to have witnessed you listen to other more insignificant topics of conversation with your full interest before they are willing to share something with you that is more emotionally weighted. If they sense you are too distracted, or perhaps too stressed, they may not want to add to the other things you have on your mind.

CONNECT FIRST WITH YOURSELF

Setting the foundation to listen fully to your child includes being able to address your own unfinished emotional business. As a conscious parent, you know that unfinished business can interfere with your ability to listen fully to your child. For example, your child may say something that triggers a response in you that comes out and takes over what your child is trying to tell you. It is in these moments that your child's needs are left unheard. If this happens, be forgiving of yourself. It's okay to go to your child later and say "I'm sorry I responded like that. I was having some of my own feelings and they took over. I'm ready to talk to you now so that I can focus on your feelings."

Are you at peace with *your* authentic self? Are you allowing yourself to be your true self, or do you feel you are regularly trying to be someone you're not? Being your own authentic self enables you to consciously listen to what your child is trying to tell you, and encourages them to be their authentic self.

Open Communication

Keeping open communication between yourself and your child sets the stage for increased honesty and trust. It's impossible to be truly connected to your child without open communication. Not only is this an essential part of parenting in general but it is essential when trying to gauge your child's internal experience of gender.

Often the focus of communication between parent and child is about what the child needs to be doing. The child may have tasks to do that the parent feels is their role to enforce, and as a result matters of school and chores can start to take over the majority of conversations. However, when the focus of conversation is primarily about behavior or tasks, you miss out on the basic "beingness" of your child. Therefore, conscious communication with your child should always include asking about how they're feeling and inquiring about topics you know are important to them. When they seem to be struggling with something, instead of first jumping to give advice, ask what their inner voice is telling them.

KEEP IT CASUAL

When asking questions about a topic, try to keep it as casual as possible. Your child can get overwhelmed if they sense an urgency to your questioning. You may sometimes get the sense your child is deflecting your questions. This may be because your child feels the need to deflect the anxiety they sense from you. When you can keep your own feelings in check, your questions may come across as more open and allow for more authentic communication. Additionally, your child may sense that there is a specific answer you're looking for. This may or may not be true, depending on how in tune you are with your own projections. Try to ask questions as casually as possible, and with a lighthearted tone. Similarly, respond casually to what they reveal. Your child will be less apt to shut down when they sense you are not having an intense emotional response to what they are telling you.

In the grand scheme of things, most conversations and situations are not emergencies. We as parents tend to feel the urgent need to address situations immediately, which increases our anxiety and decreases our ability to stay mindful. Knowing it is best for your child to approach topics with a decreased sense of urgency may help remind you that most issues are not in fact urgent. Maintaining a nonurgent posture will leave you more open for authentic feelings associated with the present moment as they reveal themselves. For example:

Child: "Ava didn't want to play with me today."
Parent: "Oh, really? How come?"

Because you didn't respond with urgency, your child will likely not absorb and adopt a sense of urgency about the situation. Additionally, you allowed space for your child to answer authentically and assess their own emotions about the situation, rather than taking on your emotions or feeling as though a certain response is expected.

MORE QUESTIONS THAN ANSWERS

When discussing something important, make sure you are asking more questions than you are giving answers. This will give you a sense of how much your child already understands about the topic, and how they feel about it. If you jump in right away with solutions, your child will miss the opportunity to share feelings, problem-solve, and form their own opinion of the situation. Questions can also be good when you aren't sure of what to say.

Additionally, asking more questions than giving answers is a way of honoring your child's internal wisdom. Knowing they are their own being and capable of free thought will help you to have the motivation to learn how they feel about something. This means that you will be less likely to try to simply instruct them or give them all the answers. For example:

Child: "Do you think I will get teased if I wear this skirt to school?"
Parent: "I'm not sure, what do you think?"

ASK OPEN-ENDED QUESTIONS

Most parents know what kind of answers they get when they ask closed questions: "yes," "no," "nothing," "fine." These answers do little to give you insight about what may be going on in the internal world of your child.

Additionally, closed questions tend to be leading, in that they can contain an answer within themselves. This means your child can either confirm or deny what you are asking without having to come up with their own original content of how to answer. (See the following examples.)

You may have a preconceived notion of what went on when you question your child, but try to avoid leading questions. If not, the chances of your child saying "yes" are high, even when it is not accurate. This is not your child trying to lie to you; such a response is often related to them trying to please you, trying to make sense of the situation, trying to avoid a hard conversation, and so forth. Here are some examples of closed and open questions:

Closed: Did you play with Andrew at recess today?
Open: What was recess like for you today?

Closed: Are you nervous about the talent show?
Open: How are you feeling about the talent show?

Closed: Did Andrew talk to you today?
Open: Who did you talk with the most today?

Closed: Did you get upset when you found out about your teacher's vacation?
Open: How do you feel about your teacher's vacation?

Other examples of open-ended questions are:

O "What makes you think that?"

O "How did that make you feel?"

O "What do you think?"

O "Why do you think someone would do/say that?"

O "What do you think you should do about that?"

O "How do you think the other person was feeling?"

The following is a set of sample dialogues between a parent and child. In the closed-ended dialogue, notice how the child responds. In contrast, notice that the open-ended questions help the parent discover what is truly bothering their child.

Closed-ended dialogue:

Parent: "What was the worst part of your day?"
Child: "Jake teasing me about my backpack."
Parent: "Well, did you tell him you didn't like that?"
Child: "Yeah."
Parent: "Good. You tell him boys can carry 'My Little Pony' backpacks, too!"
Child: "Okay."

Open-ended dialogue:

Parent: "What was the worst part of your day?"
Child: "Jake teasing me about my backpack."
Parent: "How did you feel when he did that?"
Child: "Mad."
Parent: "What made you mad about that?"
Child: "Yesterday he said he was my friend. Today he was just being mean."
Parent: "That sounds confusing. What did you do?"
Child: "I went and played with Sarah. She's always nice to me."

NONVERBAL COMMUNICATION

As much as *what* you say is important, *how* you say it and other means of nonverbal communication can be just as important. It is essential that you check in with yourself to see what you are feeling and how those feelings are driving your response to your child's communication with you. Being aware of your energy during conversations with your child is extremely important. Your child will absorb your energy to some extent, and it will impact both what they tell you and how they behave. Notice how your child reflects that energy through their behavior.

Your nonverbal communications will influence your ability to hear your child's authentic thoughts and feelings. Be mindful of what you may be saying through your facial expressions, body language, and actions.

Your child is likely very in tune with these things and may look to you for cues on how you are feeling, how they should be feeling, or how much to share.

Not only is your nonverbal communication important, so is your child's. Pay attention to your child's overall demeanor, including facial expression, body language, and "themes" of the things they are saying. Is there a pattern? Is the pattern reflective of their internal needs and motivations regarding a particular subject?

Your child may not have the words to describe their thoughts and feelings about a complex topic—including but not limited to gender—so it is important to be in tune with other ways they may be trying to communicate. If you take the time to play with your child, notice the themes of play. What are they drawing? What are they talking about the most when they are relaxed in a play mode? Are there any repeating patterns during play? What are the interactions like between the characters? This may be a window into your child's subconscious, and can give you a preview of your child's internal landscape. Children tend to "play out" issues that are either at the forefront of their minds or those which they are trying to resolve.

COMMUNICATING DURING DIFFICULT MOMENTS

It's unrealistic to think that most conversations you have with your child will be during calm, grounded times of peaceful emotions. While this type of communication is hugely important for connectedness, even more so is the way you communicate with each other during times of conflict, high emotion, and disagreement. You and your child will not always agree, and there will be times you will find yourself stretched thin on time, patience, and the ability to give your child space to just "be."

You will find yourself getting frustrated, not only because this is a natural part of life, but also because navigating the journey with your gender-expansive child can at times be frustrating. Do not feel guilty for the feelings of frustration you have about your child or their behavior. Instead, notice when these emotions come up and acknowledge their presence. What is most important is how you communicate with your child during these trying moments.

If you need a break, take one. Taking breaks is not a sign of weakness, but a sign of strength that you recognize you may be at risk for saying or doing things you might later regret. You are also modeling this coping technique for your child. Rather than "acting out" your feelings, name your feelings out loud, as this is precisely what you want your child to learn how to do. "I'm feeling really frustrated right now" or "I'm too upset to talk at the moment, let's talk in a little bit." Additionally, reflecting your child's feelings will help them learn to identify their feelings (and eventually name them). "I can see we are both feeling pretty angry right now. Let's work on calming our minds and bodies before we talk about this."

If you become anxious or angry while talking with your child, take a break. Focus on deep breathing, muscle relaxation, and changing thoughts from angry to neutral or positive before coming back together to talk. Wait to come back to talk when you are in a more grounded place, such that you are able to separate your emotions from your child and can acknowledge their feelings about the situation. A conscious parent will use empathy to resolve conflict.

If you are very frustrated and under time constraints that prevent you from taking a break and coming back to it, check in with your body to discover how much of an "emergency" the situation feels like. If it feels incredibly urgent, is it? Or is your desire to control your child or the situation engaging you in a power struggle? If you look at the situation with a different perspective, you may be able to realize there is no emergency. Relinquishing some control and lowering your anxiety will likely help you communicate better with your child in that moment.

Compassion

Compassion is a hugely important element when it comes to understanding your child's gender expansiveness and gender identity. Your role as a conscious parent is to guide your child with compassion in order for them to be a free, sovereign, and self-confident person. When you are connected to your child, it is easier to empathize with your child's point of view. When you are able to empathize with the view of others, compassion can take its complete form. For example:

O Compassion will allow you to see through any misbehaviors on behalf of your child so that you can discover the distress that is driving the behaviors.

O Compassion will help you to find the grace in every experience, and give your child grace when they need it most.

O Compassion will help you take the time to identify how your child might be feeling over the sound of your own emotions.

O Compassion will help you stay grounded even during the times when it feels like you and your child are speaking different languages.

Some parents start to feel as though they are walking on eggshells to the point that they do not say anything to offend or upset their gender-expansive youth. Have compassion for yourself as you evolve in this journey, and know their response to you has everything to do with their feelings. When you can come from a place of acknowledging their feelings rather than defending yourself, compassion has won.

In order to be more compassionate to your child, ask yourself these questions: "What is it like for my child right now? What might they be experiencing on a day-to-day basis? What can I do to respond appropriately in order to show the most compassion?" To discover the answers, you may have to be reflective and mirror what your child is feeling: "It seems as though you feel . . . ." Further, you may need to compassionately set limits: "I can see how upset you are right now, but I can't let you break things. I will help you through these big feelings."

Respect

As you likely know, respect between parent and child goes both ways. When mutual respect can be established in the parent/child dyad, it facilitates not only a more positive relationship but can also make difficult situations easier to navigate. The conscious parent acknowledges their child is their own being and has their own experiences. Too many times parents are under the illusion that they own and can control their children. In the end, your child is not yours to control or manipulate. Your responsibility is to help them be the best self they can be. Of course, this involves guidance on your part, but power should not be the main dynamic within your relationship. The crux of respect in a conscious parent/child duo will be creating a bond that instills a partnership *with* your child rather than giving you power *over* your child.

When you communicate this type of respect to your gender-expansive child, they learn to respect themselves. They also learn to expect this type of respect from others, and will therefore be more likely to stand up for themselves should they not receive it. Self-respect goes a long way in facilitating self-determination, and trusting oneself to know you are the expert on your own being.

How is respect communicated? Respect is communicated by listening to your child, honoring their unique sense of self, trusting they know themselves, and regarding them with unconditional love and acceptance. Parenting this way not only builds self-confidence but communicates a deep respect from the parent to the child. Make it your goal to respect and nurture the essential being of your child, which trumps gender and other personal traits. If you focus on relating to the essence of your child rather than the form your child takes, you will find it facilitates a natural and respectful bond.

Respect is an important element when honoring your child's gender expansiveness. By allowing them to authentically display who they are in regard to gender, you are sending the message that you respect them as a person with their own individual needs, and that you respect the unique being they are, whoever that may be.

The Foundation of Home

The home should be a safe environment for your child to be heard. Consider your home your child's "backstage." It should be a place away from the demands of outside life or constraints your child may feel in regard to their gender or gender expression. While they may monitor or conceal their true gender expression in other environments, it is important they don't do this at home. Your message at home should always be, "Any way you are is okay." Work to create a consistent, positive, nonjudgmental, loving environment your child can count on. Your child should be celebrated exactly as they are within the walls of your home. This is where self-esteem is built from the ground up. Additionally, if navigating the outside world seems tricky or scary to your child as they develop their sense of gender, having a safe home environment creates a buffer for any emotional bumps and bruises they may incur along the way.

Having an affirmative home environment that communicates unconditional love deepens your child's basic trust in the world, as well as a secure sense of self. A child who has a strong sense of self-worth will be better prepared for future challenges. The hope is that this will eventually allow them to lift the constraints they may have placed on themselves in order to be their authentic self everywhere. You, as their parent, can use this type of home environment to secure your parental influence as something to be regarded as reliable and safe.

Important Points to Consider

Being connected to your child is not only an important part of conscious parenting but is crucial on your journey with a gender-expansive child. Only when you are connected with your child will you feel confident about the direction you're headed. Here are some key concepts to keep in mind:

- O Listen carefully to your child without distraction. Filter out external obligations that pull you away from being present with your child. Your full focus will communicate value in what your child has to say, now and in the future.

- O Keep the standard of open communication between you and your child that includes asking more questions than giving answers.

- O Be mindful of both your own and your child's nonverbal communications. What might you be communicating that you don't wish to say? What might your child be trying to say but can't?

- O Empathy drives compassion, and compassion allows for understanding of what your child is going through. This, in turn, may help you better understand their behaviors and external presentation.

- O A parent/child partnership based on respect not only facilitates your relationship with your child, but also improves your child's ability to authentically explore their gender.

- O Home should be a safe place. It should be a nonjudgmental, supportive environment and it should support the authentic nature of the individuals who reside in it. This sets the stage for your child's expectations of future environments and relationships.

 **CHAPTER 4**

Foundations of Parenting

Parenting is incredible. It's likely one of the biggest honors you'll ever have in your lifetime. You get to see the evolution of a person. You get to deeply love, and be deeply loved in return. It's also one of the toughest jobs you'll ever have! Parenting is the ultimate tightrope walk. It's the constant balancing of getting tasks completed while making fond memories, facilitating a bond between yourself and your child while using guidance and discipline, and serving the needs of your child while trying to engage in self-care. Some days it may be easier to balance on that tightrope than others. When you have a gender-diverse child, the parenting tightrope walk may include some extra challenges.

Your Unique Tightrope Walk

As the parent of a gender-expansive child you must balance the unique needs of your child while paying attention to the thoughts and feelings that the child's gender expansiveness brings up in you. In addition, you must balance what your parental intuition is telling you to do while navigating the twists and turns of the impulse to prove to others that you are a "good parent." Parenting from a gender-affirmative standpoint is divisive enough of an issue that you may fluctuate from feeling like a hero to a villain depending on the source of the judgment.

If you visualize yourself on an actual tightrope, what kinds of things would help you successfully go from one end of the other without falling? These same things just may help you on the journey you're embarking on with your child. For example:

○ **Breathe.** Breathe deeply into your stomach. The more oxygen you get to your brain, the better you will be able to think. It also helps keep your body from entering "panic mode."

○ **Center yourself.** Shaking and wobbling won't do you any favors on that tightrope. You may not feel like you have firm footing, but you have resources within yourself to stabilize you. Affirm yourself, encourage yourself, and believe you can cross the rope successfully.

○ **Use help when you can get it.** Tightrope walkers often carry a balancing pole. That balancing pole is there for a reason. There are many balancing tools available to you—use them. If others are there to help support you, let them. Tell them what you need.

Let Your Child Teach You

Teaching your child is a core duty on your list of tasks when it comes to parenting. Most parents take their role as teachers very seriously. We begin teaching our children about the world almost from the minute they are born. However, authentic gender identity is one of those things you simply cannot teach. Much like you can't teach your child which eye color to have, you cannot teach them what gender identity to have. It is just something that *is*. You can teach them about how to assert their gender identity, how to cope with responses to their gender expansiveness; the list goes on and on. However, when it comes to who they are gender-wise, they have to teach you.

Your child knows who they are. Let them show you. Learn to relinquish control when it comes to this area of parenting. Yes, you still have power when it comes to making major decisions, such as medical decisions and so on. However, you cannot control your child's internal experience of gender or their inborn inclinations regarding gender expression. Only they are the expert in that.

Is supporting and allowing your child's gender expansiveness permissive parenting? No. It's important to realize the difference between managing a behavior and trying to control/ change the way your child *is*. Allowing your child to eat ice cream for dinner is a behavior. Gender identity, or how your child identifies in regards to gender, is just a way your child is.

Responding with unconditional love and acceptance in regard to how your child *is* will be the blueprint for a confident, happy, and secure individual.

"Blank Slate" Parenting

What is "blank slate" parenting? For the purpose of this book, it's the ability for a parent to enter into parenthood without too many assumptions and expectations. This may sound difficult, but it is possible. Most parents enter into parenthood with some basic assumptions: Their child is going to be cisgender, gender conforming, and heterosexual. Considering that many children are not these things, these assumptions may be inaccurate and possibly detrimental for both the parent and the child.

COMMON ASSUMPTIONS

Unless a parent is having an intersex baby, the parent will likely find out they are having an assigned male or an assigned female, either during the pregnancy or when the baby is born. Once this is revealed, all sorts of associations are created.

If the child is an assigned male, the parents will assume the child will always identify as a boy and will engage in the "typical" interests and affinities of most boys. If the child is an assigned female, the parents will assume the child will always identify as a girl and will engage in the "typical" interests and affinities of what society expects girls to be interested in. If the child is an assigned female, parents often assume they will one day be interested in males. If the child is an assigned male, parents often assume they will one day be interested in females.

Children absorb gender assumptions. Even if these assumptions are not explicitly stated, they will implicitly become the foundation of what your child understands is expected of them. Children have an inherent need to please their parents, so the actions and emotions required to break out of the mold of what is expected from them can range from uncomfortable to downright scary.

From this point of reference, anything other than what has been envisioned and assumed results in the parent needing to make a "shift" in what they had expected. The nature of this shift will depend on how tied the parents are to their expectations, and what this difference means to them personally, socially, and culturally.

SHIFTING POINTS OF REFERENCE

While being transgender, bisexual, or homosexual is not pathological, some parents will feel and/or respond as if it is. If a child was assumed to be cisgender, the discovery they are not may be quite shocking. The parents have to shift their expectations from something they thought they understood to something much different. If a child was assumed to be straight, the discovery that they are not can also be quite shocking. Even parents who consider themselves to be open-minded and okay with the possibility that their child may be gay might initially make the assumption their child is straight. Hence, the child may still have to go through a "coming out" process to explain their sexuality as if it were something variant or unexpected.

What if, instead of adopting these basic assumptions, parents remained *open* to who or what their child is or will become? What if parents provided a blank canvas for their child to paint, rather than providing a paint-by-numbers template? What if society evolved to the extent that people understood the difference between sex and gender, and the knowledge that some children are simply born transgender? Imagine how much easier it would be if parents understood not to get too attached to the sex of their child at birth! What if parents learned to ask, "Do you feel like a boy or a girl? Both, or neither?" instead of telling the child who they are based on anatomy?

What if society at large acknowledged being gay/lesbian/bisexual as a natural way to be, a way of being that is just as valid and recognized as heterosexual? What if parents learned to say "So, do you like boys or girls? Both, or neither?" instead of making assumptions of a heteronormative nature?

Here are some ways of operating from a blank slate parenting stance or creating that blank canvas for your child:

○ Instead of assuming and then waiting for them to correct you, *ask* about who your child is.

○ Expose them to and talk about diversity: different family structures, identities, and communities.

- Remind yourself often that in raising a child you should be asking them to paint a blank canvas that should turn out exactly as *they* want it to. You should not be providing a format in which they need to stay within the lines.

- Be aware of language. Avoid using the gender dichotomy like "boys and girls." Do not use strongly gendered language to refer to your child and others. Incorporate many gender-neutral phrases and expressions to allow more space for your child to decide how they relate to gender.

Parenting from a blank slate standpoint would essentially eliminate the "coming out" process. Children would be able to evolve and share as their identities developed. They would not have to hide parts of who they are for fear they might be disappointing their parents. They would not have to overcome the expectations/assumptions that were placed on them at birth.

Rather than making assumptions, ask questions, often and early, to help learn who your child is. The questions will serve two purposes: You will learn about your child, and your child will learn that there is a beautiful spectrum of human diversity, not just regulated boxes into which one has to fit.

In order to provide a blank slate for your child so that they can be free to display their authentic self, you must be mindful of your own projections and assumptions. Such things impede the ability of your child to have an actual *blank* slate on which to create. Recognize your child as their own individual being, and that you are lucky to witness their true self unfold. By asking questions about what gender they feel like on the inside, and who they like, you are demonstrating to them that you are not making assumptions. You are communicating there are several different ways to be, and that you are open to all of them. No matter how they answer the questions, respond in an affirming way. Remember the message should *always* be "Any way you are is okay."

In order to access your most conscious self while having these conversations, be mindful of distractions. Make sure you have your undivided attention on your child so that you can fully listen to and absorb what your child has to say. Allow your child to communicate about their internal self without receiving a judgmental response from you. Likewise, allow your own feelings to come and go in response to your child's answers without acting on them or being ruled by them.

Examining Personal Biases

Assuming you weren't raised by parents who were in the blank slate frame of mind, you likely entered life exposed to a set of expectations that you had to live up to. This presumably not only molded how much you were willing to share, but how you thought and felt about gender, sexuality, and the like. You also probably entered into parenthood with extensive biases about gender. These biases could have been created by both implicit and explicit gender "rules" in your family of origin.

Consider the following questions to help you explore any potential biases:

○ What did you observe in regard to gender roles in your family of origin?

○ If there were siblings of different genders, did your parent(s) treat them differently?

○ Do you remember being told you could not do something because of your gender?

○ Do you remember how others responded to you if you went outside of your expected gender role?

○ How were you reinforced for staying within your gender role, even if the response was subtle?

○ Do you feel like you met your parent(s)' expectations they may have created before your birth?

All of these things—and more—created the foundation of your understanding of gender and the "rules" that govern gender. You may still be closely tied with some of the rules communicated to you in your childhood, or you may be evolving in your own understanding of gender.

Evaluate the family rules about gender that were communicated to you either implicitly or explicitly while you were growing up. Decide which ones are functional and helpful to you or your child now, and discard the rest. Decide how you want to communicate about gender to your own child and the next generation. Conceptualize this foundation as something to build upon, although you may need to evaluate the foundation to see what parts need some major repair in order for you to be the best advocate for your gender-expansive child. No matter where your starting point is, change is always possible.

YOUR RELATIONSHIP WITH GENDER

Depending on your own gender identity and/or your own gender expression as a child, gender may have been something you spent very little time thinking about. This may be because your gender presentation was in line with what others expected, or because others responded to your gender expression in a fluid, accepting manner. If gender was never really an issue for you as a child, you may find yourself feeling surprised at how much of a center stage it takes in your child's life. You may find yourself frustrated because you can't understand. You may find yourself sad and wishing you could make your child's experience different. It's important to remember that you didn't have to have the same experience with gender as your child in order to support your child now. You are both your own beings, with your own relationship with gender; let your child teach you about theirs so you can advocate for them and understand better.

Conversely, gender may have been something you found distressing or confusing. You may have figured out coping skills (healthy or unhealthy) to deal with this. You may have figured out a way to repress your own authentic gender experience. Parents with this history and a gender-expansive child of their own may have a complicated relationship with their child's gender diversity. You may (even subconsciously) expect your child to utilize the same repressive techniques you did, and feel somewhat disappointed when they do not. You may expect your child to learn to cope with the discomfort of their assigned gender at birth, much as you did. You may feel somewhat of a vicarious release watching your child assert themselves and their gender if this was something you were never able to personally do yourself.

No matter what relationship you had with gender as a child (which morphed into your ideas about gender as an adult), all of these things influence your parenting experience. They may mold the way you communicate regarding gender roles to your child. Consider the following:

- How are gender roles communicated in your family now?

- Can you recall any gender rules you may have verbally communicated to your child in the past?

- What kinds of gender roles are modeled in your home?

- What kind of response do you model in regard to gender-expansive people, either your child or others?

- Do you feel like you reinforce (either accidentally or purposefully) staying within specific gender boundaries?

If you feel you have adhered to a set of "rules" that no longer benefit yourself or your child, know that it's never too late to evolve and shift your way of looking at things. If you feel you have said or done things that may have been damaging to the self-esteem of your gender-expansive child, take the time to apologize and show you mean it by changing your point of reference.

PARENTING BLUEPRINTS

How you were raised in regard to gender and how you view gender now may also impact the "gut reaction" you have to witnessing your child's expression of gender and/or gender identity. Pay attention to that gut reaction: What is it telling you? Is it telling you someone is "breaking the rules"? If yes, does this come from the gender rules communicated to you from your upbringing? Is it coming from the feeling that others will not approve of your child's expression/identity, or accuse you or them of some-how breaking gender rules? Is it coming from your own personal feelings about gender?

Take a minute and address that part of you that may be responding in a negative way to your child's communication of gender. Your reactions are not something to be repressed; rather they are something that should be up for an internal conversation. Many people, through insightful reflection, have actively worked to change their biases regarding gender and have reoriented themselves when it comes to this topic.

Some parents respond to their child's gender expansiveness much differently than their own parents would have. This may be a reflection of evolving times, different temperaments, or a result of a conscious effort to understand gender in ways that previous generations did not.

Whatever gender blueprint you are operating from as a parent, part of a conscious parent's task is to be aware that the blueprint exists. Without understanding what guides your thoughts and feelings about something, you may begin operating on impulse. It's important to consider and examine factors that may complicate or impede your ability to mindfully parent your gender-expansive child. Some gender structures created in childhood need a remodel, while others require a complete teardown.

Coparenting

Remember the parenting tightrope mentioned in the beginning of the chapter? Well, now picture it on a single rope with a partner, holding onto the same balancing pole and relying on each other in order to not fall off. What if you both had different ideas about how to stay on that rope? Worse yet, what if you each had a different idea about to which end of the rope you were headed?

GENDER AND COPARENTING

Coparenting can be tough for a lot of different reasons, but coparenting a gender-diverse child can bring on additional challenges. Each parent comes into the relationship with their own history, their own gender identity, their own ideas about gender and gender roles, and their own personal biases based on their culture, generation, and families of origin. Given all of these factors, it's next to impossible that both parents are going to agree completely on how to navigate their child's gender journey. *How* you handle the differences in opinion will ultimately have the greatest impact on how peacefully you experience parenting your child with unique needs and how well your partnership survives.

You may find yourself in the position of having a partner who largely thinks the way you do about parenting, gender, and the like. Or, you may find yourself disagreeing dramatically with the way your partner handles your child's gender expansiveness. You may be in the difficult position of balancing the fragility of your child's self-esteem and mental health while balancing the seeming fragility of your partnership.

Pull your partner toward you, rather than pushing them away. Ultimately, if you can support your child as a united front, then you will be doing what is best for your child. It will also be beneficial to *you* to have the support in the journey. Part of pulling your partner toward you is validating their concerns while sharing your own perspective.

If both parents feel passionately about how to raise their child and how to respond to gender expansiveness, the journey can get a bit rocky if these ideas differ. Who decides which way to go? Whose ideas take precedence? This can be difficult to decide, especially when both partners feel they are acting in their child's best interest. Perhaps you and your partner need to come together to refocus on what is most important to you both. Hopefully, you will agree your priority is to be nurturing, affirming parents with deliberate intention and awareness about what brings your child the most happiness. Visualize that tightrope. When you have the impulse to yank the balancing pole from your partner's grip and march forward in your own direction, think again. Having two sets of hands on that balancing pole may be better than one.

Take a break from this complicated dance with your partner and look at your child, your child's mood, and your child's behavior. What are these things like when *your* parenting ideas regarding gender are implemented? What are these things like when your partner takes the parenting lead? When does your child seem most content? Watch for signs of distress. If your parenting guidance is resulting in your child showing distress, take a step back. Re-evaluate the motivations for your interventions: Are they for you or your child? Are they for your child or others? When it comes to nurturing your child's authentic self, check in with yourself to make sure that your intentions are geared toward what gives your child the most space to be themselves. If your child is more at peace with your parenting guidance and shows distress when your partner takes the reins, this may indicate *you* are on the right track. Try to engage your partner in this most important practice of watching for signs of distress. One goal that can likely be agreed upon is that you both want your child in minimal distress.

APPLYING MINDFULNESS

If your partner is in disagreement with your choices, and if this disagreement results in distress for your child, you may feel as though you have to "choose" between your child and your partner. Instead, try to think about it less as choosing your child, and more about the fact that your child *is* a child! Your child relies on you for safety, comfort, guidance, and emotional security. If your child's other parent is making decisions that go against these things, it is imperative to set some firm boundaries. Your partner is an adult and is better able to handle conflict when things are not going their way. Your partner may need you, but differently. Encourage them to engage in their own self-care and reach out to others for support.

One parent may be more aware of their own biases and be more mindful of their own gut reactions in regard to their child's expression. Is this a conversation you and your partner can have? Would you and your partner be willing to agree that if one parent experiences a strong, complicated reaction to your child's behavior, they will "tap out" and let the other parent step forward? This is certainly a tricky strategy, and it requires a great deal of mindfulness. Each of you checking in with yourself in quiet moments is essential to knowing where you stand in more chaotic moments that require quick decisions. It is essential for each parent to be engaging in enough self-care that there is a strong foundation from which to operate. It will be difficult to consciously parent if there are strong unmet needs in the moment. Additionally, parents will need to identity what triggers them into being pulled into a less conscious frame of mind, and then work on resolving this.

Having a discussion to redefine the mutual goals of parenting may be helpful if your partner is struggling. Do you notice your partner trying to control your child or their gender expression? Is there a way to refocus on more conscious ways of parenting, such as nurturing and partnering with the child rather than controlling? Remind your child's other parent that trusting your child to know themselves is essential for creating a confident, happy human being.

BALANCING BLENDED FAMILIES

In a blended family, a child's gender journey may be influenced by many individuals. Open communication and collaboration are ideal, but not always attainable in these situations. Try to remain mindful of your child's feelings, and also be aware of the feelings that come up in you when you see others influencing the journey. You may not be able to control what is said or done in another household where your child spends time. If you perceive something to be damaging to your child, your child's self-esteem, or your child's ability to be recognized for their true self, speak up and intervene. If what is happening in the other home is different than your own home but is not likely damaging, talk to your child about it. Ask questions about how it makes them feel, why they think it is like that at the other house, and so on. Stay in the present moment with your child instead of the past in regard to your relationship with the coparent. Work on equipping your child with coping skills for either dealing with challenges at the other environment or for positively asserting themselves and their gender expression/identity.

Your Child's Unique Gender Journey

While there are books and support groups that provide some guidance on how to navigate a child's gender-expansive journey, you may find yourself wishing there was a "how to" manual specifically for *your* child's journey. You may look to other parents in the community in an effort to learn from their experiences. This can be invaluable. Other parents who have walked in similar shoes can be your greatest resource and your biggest supporters. However, resist the urge to compare the steps and stages of one child's journey with experiences of your child's. Just when the two journeys are sounding similar, inevitably there will be one key difference that plants doubts in your head. "My kid isn't like that/doesn't do that, so I wonder if . . . ." Keep in mind that no gender-expansive or transgender child is the same. While the journey of another child may have some striking similarities to that of your child, remain open to the fact that your child's story is uniquely their own.

There is no singular trajectory that all gender-expansive/ transgender children take. All children are different in regard to their developmental stages, temperaments, personalities, academic performance, athletic abilities, and so on. The same is true for gender-expansive and transgender children.

One gender-expansive child may be diverse in most facets of their life; others may be diverse in just one. One transgender child may express their "true" gender very early on, while others are not consciously aware of this until much later. Some children will readily show and tell their parents exactly who they are and what they want to do about it. Others (usually depending on temperament) may show signs of who they are and what they want but won't assert themselves. In this type of circumstance, it can be helpful for parents to ask questions and open up the lines of communication around the subject of gender. Ask specific questions about their gender identity, and how they want to be regarded by others. You do not need to be afraid that asking questions will "plant ideas" or "push" your child into feeling a certain way or doing something that is not natural to them. You will simply be creating an environment where your child feels free to be open with you, even if they need to be nudged to do so.

THE GENDER CLUB

If your child is gender-expansive, then you are part of the Gender Club! You may have been in the Gender Club for a long time, or you may only now just have joined. People can join the Gender Club in any number of ways and for any number of reasons. One may join the Gender Club by being gender-expansive themselves. One may join by loving someone who is gender-expansive, which facilitates a need to learn more about gender than one previously knew or understood. A person can even join the Gender Club through the work they do, or through an understanding they develop over time through exposure to diversity, social interactions, education, or life circumstances. Whatever way you come into the Gender Club, once you're in it there's really no going back. Once you understand certain basics about gender, gender expression, and gender expansiveness, there is no unlearning this. And that is a good thing.

Members of the Gender Club understand the difference between gender and sex. They understand not everyone feels the same gender identity as their assigned gender at birth. They understand there are a myriad of combinations of gender expression and identities. They understand that there are not just boys and girls, and that there is no such thing as "boy toys" and "girl toys." They understand the pronouns someone asks for are the very pronouns that make them feel recognized as their authentic self.

However, many other people you interact with may not be in the Gender Club. In fact, a lot of the opinions and advice you receive from others regarding how to parent your gender-expansive child may be from people outside of the Gender Club. This can be difficult to tolerate. You may hear them reinforcing gender stereotypes either to your child or in general. They may not understand when you try to explain your child to them. Remind yourself they are not in the Gender Club. Not yet.

Those of us in the Gender Club are pioneers. We are forging the way for the rest of society, and are making the world safer for gender-expansive individuals. We are changing the way society looks at gender, understands gender, and embraces gender—and there are more members joining every day.

Important Points to Consider

Parenting can feel like walking a tightrope. Stay focused on the end goal, center yourself, and utilize the help available to you. Attempt to parent from a place of curiosity; watch to see how your child will develop and grow. Try to avoid having a very specific end result or mold that you want your child to fit into. Here are some other important things to remember:

O Be aware of how your own personal history, temperament, and life experience affect you and your ideas about gender and what you expect from your child based on their assigned gender at birth. Evaluate whether or not these ideas remain functional in your current place and time, as well as how they are affecting your child.

O Even if you didn't start this way, try to approach parenting now with a blank slate of mind. Know that you are privy to the unfolding of an individual; remain curious how that individual will turn out without projecting expectations.

O Be mindful of how you are handling disagreements, if they exist, regarding gender and gender expression with the coparent of your child. Are you each able to check in with your personal biases and how they affect your decisions? Are each of you able to be aware of what minimizes your child's distress and act accordingly? Do you feel you are pulling each other in when you disagree, or are you pushing each other away? Even blended families can work well together for the sake of the gender-expansive child if all parties focus on the same goal: the child's happiness.

○ Just as fingers resemble each other but fingerprints are each intricately different, such is the same with your child's gender journey. Your child will certainly have similarities with other children on a gender-expansive path, but the details will be distinctly unique.

○ Your child will need to guide you in understanding their needs when it comes to gender/gender expression. Allowing them to "be" a certain way is entirely different from allowing behavior they can choose.

○ Now that you are in the Gender Club, use it to your child's advantage. Welcome others into the club by teaching them to let go of previously held assumptions about gender.

CHAPTER 5

Parenting the Gender-Expansive Child

Parenting a gender-expansive child can be fun and delightful in a lot of aspects. Your gender-expansive child may open your eyes and your heart in ways you never expected. You may feel liberated from previously held gender "rules," and you may connect with other amazing people who understand or can relate to gender expansiveness. Also, parenting a gender-expansive child can present some unique challenges. The parent of a gender-expansive child may find themselves in a complicated mesh of worrying about their child and how society will respond to them, as well as feeling as though they too don't "conform" to what is typically expected of a parent in regard to raising a child.

Needs of the Gender-Expansive Child

If your child engages in play, dress, or interests that society does not typically categorize as that of their assigned gender, let them. This behavior could mean any number of things, but the most important message to send your child is "Any way you are is okay." Some parents worry about future teasing, and discourage them from engaging in behaviors to prevent teasing in other environments. However, establishing pure and unconditional acceptance at home is the most crucial part of growing up. This gives them the foundation of confidence and self-esteem on which they will build the needed coping skills to deal with outside influences.

> The fewer expectations and gender rules your child feels they have to adhere to, the more space there will be for your child's unique and authentic expression of self.

Just as everything exists on a spectrum, needs of the gender-expansive child can be very unique depending on each individual. Some children are very confident and have few inhibitions regarding their gender expression. They will dress as and play with whatever they choose, regardless of any gender roles or rules they have been exposed to, and regardless of others' reactions. Other children will be quite different and will have extensive inhibitions, causing them to pick and choose what they wear and how they play based on the audience and the environment. Some of these children may hear a limitation about what they "should" be like early on, and tuck it away inside as a constant reminder to filter their behavior.

A BLANK CANVAS YOUR CHILD CAN PAINT

Ideally, children should be raised in an environment that communicates that all colors are for all children, all toys are for all children, and there are not rigid gender roles about dress and play. If this environment did not come about until after your child began showing gender-expansive behaviors, it may be time to re-address some things that may have previously been implicitly or explicitly communicated to your child. Share your thoughts about gender and gender expression, letting them know how your thoughts and feelings may have evolved to how you feel now. It may sound something like this:

- "I know before I said girls don't have short hair, but I now realize everyone should pick their own haircut style. Short hair is for kids who like short hair!"

- "I know before I said boys don't paint their nails, but I now realize anyone who wants to should paint their nails. I can see how happy it makes you!"

- "I know before I said girls should know how to cook, but I now realize that was silly; *everyone* might want to learn how to cook!"

Depending on temperament, inhibitions, anxiety, personality, and other factors, your child may need to be reminded several times. Communicate these beliefs with your words and model it with your behavior as well. As you know, children learn more by observing your behavior than by listening to the words you say.

Learn to avoid categorizing toys, occupations, colors, clothing, and the like based on gender. Have your child witness you buying a gender-neutral toy for a baby shower. Have your child hear you using gender-nonspecific words like "police officer" or "firefighter." Let your child watch you present them and their siblings with a variety of choices for birthday party themes, not just those typically designated for children of a specific gender.

BE PREPARED

You may need to decide specific words to use to describe your child's gender expansiveness to others. If this is something that makes you feel awkward, being prepared will help you communicate more self-assuredness to the other person. Most important, your child may be listening or watching you explain this. Own it, so your child can, too.

Prepare in advance how you would respond to questions or responses to your child's gender expansiveness. For example:

○ "That's her style, and I love it."

○ "In our house, we believe all colors are for all kids."

○ "I know, he's rocking that dress, isn't he?"

Similarly, your child may need to be given words in order to respond to others' questions or comments. You can find your child's favorite responses by discussing and exploring this with them, depending on the ones they feel best about. Some children seem to feel most comfortable saying something like "I am a boy who likes girl things" or "I'm a girl who likes boy things." These are not ideal as they reinforce the gender dichotomy (and gender stereotypes), but some children seem to be most comfortable using this terminology because it's something they know their peers will understand. Other examples may include:

○ "Everyone gets to pick their own style."

○ "That's just what I like."

○ "All toys are for all kids."

○ "There's no such thing as a boy thing or a girl thing."

The biggest and most important need for a gender-expansive child is unconditional acceptance. This begins at home. When those raising a child are not fully accepting, the child does not learn to be fully accepting of themselves. Work rigorously to create an environment that is loving and accepting so your child knows how to do that for themselves. Whether it be explicitly stated or conveyed through nonverbal expression, find ways to communicate "Any way you are is okay."

Your Emotional Response

It is important to get in touch with your own motives and feelings in order to understand how they may impact your parenting, particularly when it comes to your child's gender-expansiveness. Your emotional response will depend on many personal factors. These factors include but are not limited to your personality, temperament, religious affiliations, culture, family of origin, geographical location, and your own relationship with gender. Your internal characteristics will interact with the external factors in your life to create an individualized experience that is elicited by your child's gender-expansiveness. Like most other things, your emotional response to your child's gender expansiveness may also be on a spectrum. It may change day to day, or it may evolve over time.

MINDFULLY ACCEPTING YOUR RESPONSE

No matter what emotions arise, it will be most beneficial to you if you are able to accept them. Resisting your emotions and trying to suppress them increases stress and decreases quality of life. Additionally, trying to escape from your emotions makes you less consciously aware. When you are able to understand why you are feeling a certain way, your consciousness level rises.

Remember that we are all social beings who are all impacted by our environment. We have all been socialized to want to conform, or fit in, and it's natural that you as a parent should want your child to do the same. One of the most valuable things your child's gender journey can teach you is that there are more important things in life than conforming!

You may have already formed an opinion about gender normative roles before you had children, either assuming your child would be gender conforming or planning on how you would respond if they were not. Regardless of how much preparation you might have done in your head, your actual response may surprise you. You may believe with your whole heart that it is fine for children to be gender-expansive, that there is no one way to be a boy or a girl, and that you know it is in their best interest to allow them to be exactly who they are. However, external factors may play with your response and emotions more than you might expect. You may find yourself worrying more about what others think of your gender-expansive child than you did in your pre-parenting fantasies. You may feel embarrassed, protective, confused, or a combination of all when your child expresses an interest in dressing or engaging in behaviors that are typically associated with another gender.

Additionally, you may feel your child is a reflection on you and therefore you may feel as though you don't fit in when your child is different. You may be angry at yourself or feel guilty for this response. Please don't. Be kind to yourself. No matter where you fall on the spectrum of acceptance, don't judge yourself for having feelings about this. Know that any way you feel about this is okay, but the most important thing is how you manage those feelings and parent your child.

Rather than shaming or repressing the part of you that is struggling emotionally with your child's gender expansiveness, invite it in without judgment. Nurture yourself and any unpleasant feelings that may arise from your initial emotional response. Remind yourself that you are human, and that feelings come and go as they will. Your love for your child will show through based on how you act upon these feelings as well as how selective you are about sharing them with your child. It is important to understand that your feelings are something you should address on your own and/or with other adults, without your child knowing too much about your emotional response to their gender expansiveness.

FORGIVE YOURSELF

Early in the days of your child's gender expansiveness, you may have not been self-aware enough or informed enough to respond in a way you can now feel proud of. Many parents begin this journey by saying or doing things that they may later cringe about after they better understand gender identity or their child's gender expansiveness. Again, be kind to yourself. Remind yourself that you did not know then what you know now and you were doing the best you could at that time. Forgive yourself if you need to. Being compassionate and forgiving to yourself helps you to become a more conscious person. Negative thoughts and feelings you may hold about yourself actively work against being mindful in the moment. Let them go so you can have a greater chance at happiness as you remain present for your child.

If your child is old enough to understand and remember something that was once said in an attempt to extinguish their gender-expansive behaviors, have a conversation about it. Share what is in your heart and what you can remember saying, and how you now realize that was not the best thing to do. Ask your child how they were impacted by your words or behaviors. Apologize and comfort if necessary, and then move forward.

AFFIRMATIONS

Try these affirmations to support yourself in this journey:

- ○ I choose to accept not only my child's gender expansiveness, but also my own spontaneous emotional response to it.

- ○ I choose to allow my feelings to come and go as they will, but I commit to acting in such a way that I know is best for my child.

- ○ I choose to realize that while my role is to take care of my child and their emotions, it's okay for me to have my own emotions and to reach out for support from other adults when necessary.

Society's Bias

Society has a much greater tolerance for assigned females to express masculinity than it does for assigned males to express femininity. There's a wide range of theories for why this is, but most important is how it may affect you and your gender-expansive child. If your child is an assigned male who is feminine or prefers activities or interests that are deemed to be feminine, they have likely received some pushback either at home or in society, or both. There is a great deal of pressure placed upon assigned males to be masculine. This is demonstrated in the way society responds to assigned males being emotional or cheerful, showing affection toward other boys, or being sensitive. Language is used to both tease and encourage males, such as "boys don't cry," "man up," "don't be a sissy," "you throw like a girl," and so on.

All of these expressions try to use shame to mold an assigned male into being a person who is tough, unemotional, and good at sports. That's a pretty narrow range of expectations. If your child is an assigned male who is gender-expansive, check in to see if you have any former bias that inadvertently may be getting triggered. Remind yourself that even if your child is going against what society has set for expectations of their assigned gender at birth, you don't have to buy in. Gender expansiveness is not pathological. Some kids are gender-expansive, and some kids are not. Your child is okay any way they are. You need to believe this in order to genuinely communicate it to your child. If this doesn't feel authentic at first, give it time. You will evolve. Working against messages that may have been taught to you your whole life will take some time to reprogram. Remind yourself of your parenting goals: Do they focus on having a child who is happy, or a child who conforms?

If you are tempted to modify the gender expression of your child to "help them avoid getting teased," think again. This desire almost certainly comes from a place of love and protectiveness. However, by doing this you will inadvertently be sending messages you likely want to avoid: "You are not okay just the way you are," and "How society thinks of you is more important than your own authentic self and happiness." Since teasing may be common for gender-expansive children (particularly assigned males), that is what has to change, not your child.

If your child is an assigned female who is masculine in gender presentation and expression, they have likely been given more leeway in society in regard to being masculine. They may be affectionately referred to as a "tomboy," and they are likely to get far less pushback when picking masculine clothing or haircuts as compared to their gender-expansive assigned male cohort. However, you may have your own adjusting to do. What were your expectations of having a child assigned female at birth? How did you expect them to dress or act? If you feel the urge to mold them into either the child you expected or one who acts like a gender conforming girl, resist. "Molding" in this scenario can create self-doubt, a desire to please others over one's self, and sends the message that one should avoid listening to their inner voice.

Holidays and Celebrations

Holidays and other big celebrations can be particularly tricky for the gender-expansive child and their family. While you undoubtedly hope that holidays and celebrations will be happy occasions, the dynamics inherent in not conforming to society's expectations of gender can make these special occasions unhappy, disappointing, or uncomfortable for your gender-expansive child.

Depending on the culture and/or geographical location of your family, there may be fairly rigid gender-expectations when it comes to holidays and dressing formally. If your culture places value on gender-specific "fancy" garb, your gender-expansive child may bristle at the idea of wearing the outfit that is prescribed to them. Many parents of gender nonconforming youth can find themselves in a battle on special occasions over getting their child to wear something that is expected for their assigned gender at birth.

> If your priority is your child's happiness and you want to feel connected to your child, take steps to help that goal become a reality for that specific holiday. This may include changing plans or paving the way for your child on the special day. Remember that making some concessions in regard to tradition or clothing is far less important than your child's sense of self.

If this is you, take the time to stop and check in with yourself. Try to get in touch with the purpose of the holiday. Is it a time for family members to feel closer than usual? Is it a time to take a break from the rigors of daily life and connect and celebrate with loved ones? It likely is. These priorities should take precedence over getting your child to subscribe to a gender role that was written before their own unique self even existed.

Take specific steps to avert difficult situations by planning ahead. Do you need to alert family members in advance about what your child will be wearing to avoid questions or confrontations on the day of the actual holiday? Do you need to fiercely decide to resist pressure from society and family members to force your child to wear something they do not want to wear? Do you need to make some choices about who you will be celebrating with or where you will be celebrating? Take the steps you need to protect your enjoyment of and your child's happiness on the occasion.

GIFTS

Gifts, which are meant to be the source of joy and appreciation, can conversely become a source of bitter disappointment for the gender-expansive child. If the gift-giver is unaware of or resistant to your child's gender expression or preferences, their gift may range from something your child simply doesn't want to conveying a message to your child that says "What you like is not okay; this is what I think you should like."

Prepare your child in advance for how to respond if given a gift that is definitely outside of their preferences. Communicate that some people may not know what they like, and so may choose gifts that are not ideal. You can let your child know what to say, such as a simple thank you, and then assure them there will be the opportunity to return or exchange an item for something more in line with their preferences.

Decide what needs to happen so that your child can be blessed with things that are not only in line with what they want but that send the message "Anything you like is okay." Do you need to send an e-mail to family members explaining the types of gifts your child would like? Avoid using the phrase that your child likes "girl things" or "boy things" to avoid reinforcing the gender dichotomy. Instead, be specific: "Joseph likes princesses, purses, anything that sparkles, and the color purple." A wish list with specific items on it may help. If you are throwing your child a birthday party and classmates are to attend, be specific about your child's wishes on the invitation. "Sarah's current interests are: all things Spider-Man, monster trucks, Star Wars, Lego, and the color green." Some parents may suggest gender-neutral gifts, such as art supplies, movies, outings, and so on.

Avoid using apologetic language or acting as though your child's interests are something to be even remotely shameful about. "Just to warn you, Joseph will have a princess cake at the party!" This communicates embarrassment and will be absorbed by your potential party guest. Instead, own it. If you feel your potential guests may act inappropriately if surprised by a princess cake, you can say something like "Joseph is looking forward to seeing you at his party, and the 'pièce de résistance,' a princess cake!"

Responding to Difficult Situations

Even if you take the steps to be proactive and prepare others and your gender-expansive child, inevitably there may be some difficult circumstances to navigate. You may experience many different and varied circumstances, so instead of trying to anticipate all possible scenarios, focus instead on the core features of your responses. When emotions run high, be it anxiety, disappointment, anger, and so on, your main task at hand is to stay present with yourself and with your child.

Remind yourself your feelings are valid. They do not rule you or your responses, rather they are there to remind you of how important the situation is. Teach your child the same: Feelings are feelings; they will come and go as situations change. You both can handle any feeling that comes your way.

Calm your body down if it is revved up in response to the situation or the emotions associated with it. The slower and more relaxed your body is, the calmer your brain will be. The clear thinking that results will help you process the situation rationally. If there is another person involved (loved one or stranger, purposefully or inadvertently), you may need to help your child understand that some people don't understand gender as much as you both do, and that there really aren't gender rules even though other people think so.

Remind yourself of your main goals when confronted with difficult situations. You want your child to feel safe. You want your child to feel happy. You want your child to feel they are okay any way they are.

Friendship Challenges

In childhood, friendships and the art of establishing friendships evolve as children grow from simple to more complex. Think of how easy it is to make a friend as a young child. Often it's as straightforward as "Do you want to play?" or "Do you want to be my friend?" Connections are made easily, conflicts are forgiven quickly, and idiosyncrasies of friends are either not noticed or embraced. At this developmental stage, gender does not play much of a part in the friendships. Children are aligned by similar interests, and a group of girls will easily accept a boy into their group if the boy wants to play what they are playing.

As children get older, two things happen: Friendships become more complex, and children become more aware of the gender dichotomy (not only "boys and girls" but "boys versus girls"). Making friends is not as easy as it once was. Some friendships are already established, making forging new bonds more difficult. Conflict or disagreements can cause problems that last for days or weeks, or even cause friendships to end. As children get older they become more interested in conforming, and they will quickly reject a peer who does not conform or allow them to fit in. A group of girls will no longer accept a boy in their midst, citing "no boys allowed." The gender-expansive male may then have difficulty connecting to others, as their male peers may not be welcoming to him or be interested in things that he has no interest in.

Parents can attempt to assist their child in navigating these challenges. Continue to encourage your child if they get discouraged about not being included in certain groups. Coach your child to try to establish some one-on-one friendships based on interests and personality types. Perhaps emphasize this approach more so than strategies for trying to fit in with a group of kids. Arrange for times for your child to socialize with peers one-on-one outside of school time, based on mutual interests. This creates a bond between children that can help foster closer relationships at school.

Important Points to Consider

Your child should be allowed to freely express themselves in regard to their gender, and not have to choose preferences based on their assigned gender at birth. As a conscious parent who wants to help your child be their true self, remember the following:

○ Establishing that there are no gender "rules" is beneficial for your child and contributes to a larger societal shift.

○ Be aware of your emotional responses to your child's gender expansiveness without judgment.

○ Wanting to "fit in" yourself as a parent with other parents and society at large is a natural impulse; just remember it is not as important as your child's self-esteem or sense of self.

○ By welcoming others into knowing what your child would like as a gift and what they prefer to wear for holidays, you may worry less about responses the day of and enjoy the celebration more.

○ Part of your own self-care and the care of your child may come from preparing for and being proactive about specific situations.

○ Remain confident in your child's ability to make friends so that they pick up on this confidence from you. Help your child think of ways to connect with kids on a one-on-one basis rather than fitting into an already-established group.

CHAPTER 6

Parenting the Transgender Child

Most people know what gender they are from a very young age. Cisgender individuals don't have to think much about it; their sense of their gender matches their assigned sex (sex at birth) and becomes part of their stats, like where they live, what eye color they have, and so on. For transgender children, things are not so simple. They may feel a discomfort with their assigned gender, pronouns, or how they are categorized. This discomfort may first arise if they are discouraged from engaging in the interests that come naturally to them, and later may evolve into a deeper sense of personal incongruence.

Transgender versus Gender-Expansive

Gender-expansive children and transgender children have a lot in common. Their behavior, presentations, and struggles may look similar, especially when the child is younger. In the beginning it may be difficult to differentiate between a gender-expansive child and a transgender child, although often time will reveal the distinction.

At first, you may not see a transgender child speaking to their true gender identity. Because children operate with a concrete way of thinking, they are more interested in what they want to *do* and what kind of fun they want to have. They do not think abstractly about what gender or societal category they fit into.

When a gender-expansive child is not allowed to partake in an activity or interest because it is not typically seen as acceptable for their assigned gender, this can create a feeling of unrest (at best) to deep shame and resentment (at worst). This is true for both transgender children and gender-expansive children.

Being transgender goes beyond having interests or ways of expressing oneself that are not "typically" associated with their birth gender. It has more to do with feeling an incongruence between their sense of self, the gender they feel they are, and the gender assigned to them at birth (based on their external sex organs). This incongruence can lead to feelings of dysphoria. The word *dysphoria* means "a state of unease or generalized dissatisfaction with life," and comes from the Greek word *dusphoros*, meaning "hard to bear."

Gender dysphoria is a term that specifically references the feeling of unease and dissatisfaction with one's assigned gender at birth. Gender dysphoria can range from slight discomfort to intense depression. Gender dysphoria can be in regard to how one is seen by others and/or one's physical body. Some, but not all, transgender children express dissatisfaction with their physical bodies or anatomy.

WHO IS YOUR CHILD?

One way to differentiate between gender identity and gender expression is to listen closely to what your child is talking about. If your child is talking about who they are, they are referencing their gender identity. Talk about gender identity may sound something like "I wasn't supposed to be born a girl" or "I am a boy." Gender expansiveness focuses more on what they are doing; for example, what they want to play or how they wish to dress.

Some children are consciously aware of their gender incongruence from a very early age. Other children are not aware of their gender incongruence until puberty (at which time it often becomes a feeling of crisis). Additionally, some children simply don't have the verbal skills to express what they want or how badly they want it. Many people are not aware until adulthood!

One positive aspect of trying to glean a child's true gender identity is that children don't have decades of emotional baggage to carry, nor do they have the tendency to overthink the way adults do. They know what they know, and they feel what they feel. In some ways this makes expressing one's gender identity much simpler, especially if the child is in an environment that encourages natural and genuine expression of self.

Most gender-expansive children understand "the rules," and the expectations in their family/society/community/school. They may know how they feel and who they are, but most also understand what others think and what others want. Some children learn to "play the game" as we all do, giving answers to make others feel better, even when it's not the truth. Parents unknowingly ask leading questions all the time, and kids know what their parents want to hear. This can make figuring out if a child is transgender or gender nonconforming more complicated. Refer to Chapter 3 for ideas on how to ask more open-ended questions, without leading your child to an answer.

Consistent! Persistent. Insistent?

One of the cornerstone phrases for recognizing a transgender child is whether or not they have been *consistent* and *persistent* in their cross-gender identification. This means the child has shown a consistent ("unchanging in achievement or effect over a period of time") identification with a gender other than the one which they were assigned at birth, and that this has persisted ("continued to exist or endure") over a prolonged period. This applies not just to gender expression and interests but also to how they relate to themselves or identify in terms of gender.

More recently, *insistent* has been added to further qualify how a transgender child will likely present. However, the level of insistence displayed by the child is largely dependent upon the child's temperament. Not all transgender children will be insistent about their true gender.

If taking all different temperaments into consideration, we may want to also reconsider the use of the word *persistent* when it comes to transgender children. Another definition for persistent is "continuing firmly or obstinately in a course of action in spite of difficulty or opposition." Will all transgender children be persistent in this way or be insistent in the face of opposition or redirection from parents/other significant figures in their lives? Likely not.

One's personality and desire to please parents are both on a spectrum. Many children have passive personalities and so are not insistent about anything, much less their gender identity or desire to be recognized as something other than their assigned gender at birth. Some children eat their vegetables simply because they are told to. Others refuse to take even a bite despite any tactics used by those feeding them. Such is the same with gender identity.

Do not make the assumption that just because your child is not insistent upon having a different gender identity that they are not transgender.

You may miss something if you wait for this "cornerstone" of identity in transgender youth. If your child displays signs of having a different gender than assigned at birth but is not insistent upon it, continue to ask questions and communicate that you are entirely open to conversations and possibilities for ways to express one's true gender.

Some parents whose child was not gender-expansive until they were a bit older find themselves questioning the authenticity of their child's gender identification because they did not see their child being "consistent and persistent" while growing up. Just because a transgender individual does not become consciously aware of being transgender or disclose until adolescence or adulthood does not mean some of the "cornerstone" indicators weren't present. They may have simply been undisclosed. Every person has their own way of understanding and expressing their gender.

DISTRESS AND TEMPERAMENT

If a child is consciously aware of identifying with a gender other than what was assigned to them at birth (i.e., an assigned female feels like a boy, or an assigned male feels like a girl), how much they express this will depend on several factors.

One factor is the level of distress the incongruence brings them. If they find it nearly intolerable to be categorized wrong or be referred to as a gender other than their brain gender identity, they are going to be more motivated to inform those around them. Another factor is their temperament. If they have a willful, assertive, or strong personality, they are going to insist upon most things, including their gender identity.

Some children will scream "I am a boy!" or "I am a girl!" and insist upon wearing what they want, being referred to as they want, and so on until everyone around them is quite clear of who they really are. Others, if told the way they feel or how they perform gender is wrong or unexpected, will quickly make modifications to please those around them. This is not likely a reflection of how "strong" their gender identity is, rather it is a reflection of personality.

Additionally, how a child communicates that they feel like they are another gender can also be reflective of their personality and their general understanding of how things "work." In regard to possibly being transgender, some believe there is a very important distinction between a child saying "I want to be a girl" and "I *am* a girl." Many believe the latter is the statement a transgender child is more likely to use. While phrases like these may be a way to help you differentiate pretend play, imagination, and gender identity, communication choices are also likely reflective of the child's sense of the world. Some transgender children do start out by saying "I wish I was . . . ." Such a statement, however, may largely depend on the child's relationship with what they have been told to be "true" and how confident they feel to question that "truth." Their other behaviors and possible distresses will help differentiate disclosures about gender identity from imaginative play. Additionally, depending on how concrete or abstract the child is, some children simply won't say "I *am*" a boy or girl if their anatomy or others around them are telling them otherwise.

The terms *persistency* and *consistency* are typically used in regard to both gender expression and gender identification. This includes way of dress, interests, how the child seems to categorize themselves (in play, roles, or how they relate to others), gender of friends, bathroom behavior, and so on. If these things seem to be an expression of gender identification, they may be signs that the child has a gender identity that does not match their birth sex. However, the individual (a child, teen, or adult) may not be consciously aware of being transgender until much later. If the child is yet to be consciously aware that they have the brain gender identity of something other than their assigned sex at birth, there is nothing to be insistent about.

TIMING AND CAUSES OF CONSCIOUS AWARENESS

Transgender individuals become consciously aware of being so at various ages and stages; some seem to know in toddlerhood, others as children, others as soon as puberty begins, still others only in their late teens or adulthood. When this awareness occurs is largely dependent upon on how much the individual has been exposed to knowledge of variations of gender, family environment, and how freely one is allowed to express oneself in regard to gender. Defenses, including suppression and distraction, play a role in awareness (or lack thereof) as well. Only once the individual is consciously aware of being transgender does transition become a factor.

Whether the individual is a child who insists on their true gender since the time they could speak or an adult who does not become consciously aware until much later, both are equally transgender. The age of conscious awareness is simply different.

For those who were not consciously aware of being transgender in early childhood, a catalyst often triggers self-awareness. The means by which someone may be triggered into understanding their true gender identity could be other transgender people, mainstream media, books, and of course, information found on the Internet.

Some parents lament the existence of the Internet, feeling certain that if it did not exist their child would never have learned about this topic and would therefore not be transgender. The truth of the matter is that their child would still be transgender, but they may not be consciously aware of it or know what options are available to them until much later. This is not necessarily a good thing. For those who feel the need to transition, early medical intervention can be very beneficial. For those who identify as nonbinary or are otherwise under the transgender umbrella, they may come to understand their gender identity and how to ask others to respect it much earlier than they might otherwise have.

A catalyst does not *cause* the existence of something; it simply allows for awareness of something that exists. In many ways, the catalyst has an extremely important job and is an essential part of the process. Just as a menu of food choices can be the catalyst to help you recognize (and do something about) your existing hunger, such is the case with something triggering awareness of being transgender. Transgender people may be grateful to the person or medium that brought this into their conscious awareness, as understanding oneself is invaluable.

Your Child's Heart and Brain, Revealed

As previously mentioned, the language often used to discuss gender identity with children is "hearts and brains." This depiction helps a child understand whether or not they "feel and think" like a boy or a girl, or if they might be somewhere else on the spectrum. This depiction can be worded in the following way:

- ○ Some people have the hearts and brains of boys.

- ○ Some people have the hearts and brains of girls.

- ○ Some people feel like both a boy and a girl.

- ○ Some people feel like neither a boy nor a girl.

Notice the term *and* is used instead of *but*. The purpose of using *and* is to communicate the concept of "in addition to" (the term *but* communicates that the body is at odds with the brain). Looking at one's self as a whole (body and gender) normalizes that all people are simply born differently.

Gender-expansive children can complete some simple questions to communicate how they are conceptualizing their gender:

- ○ I think I have the heart of a _____. (boy, girl, or both)

- ○ I think I have the brain of a _____. (boy, girl, or both)

- ○ If I had it my way, people would treat me like a boy/girl. (Circle one or both.)

- ○ If I had it my way, people would say he/she when talking about me. (Circle one or neither. Gender-neutral pronouns are a bit advanced for younger children but can be discussed if the child communicates not relating to either "he" or "she".)

- ○ If I had it my way, people would call me _____. (preferred name)

For a copy of this worksheet with graphics, please visit *www .DarleneTandoGenderBlog.com* and search for "worksheet" in the search bar.

This work is best done with a gender therapist, as the gender therapist is not personally invested in the gender of the child. Children may worry about the response or expectations of the parent helping them complete this form. However, if you choose to do this at home, please follow these tips for completing the worksheet with your child:

O Don't make a big deal of it. Just say you're going to do a little worksheet and do it. Act like it's no big deal and show that you're not nervous, even if you are.

O Don't look at the child being interviewed. Look at the sheet of paper.

O Poise your pen or pencil over the blanks and begin asking the questions.

O Write the answer in the blank as soon as they are stated, without a reaction (facial expression or question). Children are incredibly in tune with others' responses to what they are saying, particularly if the "other" is a parent.

O When the worksheet is completed, go back and ask questions for clarification if needed, but keep these to a minimum.

Your Emotional Response

If it's becoming clear to you that your child is transgender and not "just" gender-expansive, you are likely to have a relatively strong response with a plethora of emotions. Parents typically evolve in the journey with their transgender child from tearful and terrified to peaceful and resolute. Some become advocates, others are willing to share their stories, and still others remain very private. Again, this depends on many factors including how old your child is, your personal background, your thoughts about gender, or how long you've felt (even subconsciously) aware of your child's gender conflict. The initial response can feel overwhelming, and at first many parents find themselves wanting it not to be true.

REMAIN AWARE

This time of initial realization is a moment when it is important to remain consciously aware of what is going on inside of you. This may be a time when your unconscious mind wants to take over, and if it does, your needs will feel extremely urgent. It will be hard for you to tune in with your child's needs in that moment because your feelings will take precedence. If you are able to recognize this and (rather than reacting) connect with your conscious mind, you will feel more capable of tolerating your own feelings and be present for what your child needs from you. When you are upset and your unconscious mind takes over, everything will feel personal. It may feel as though you are reacting to some sort of attack. Your child's needs are never an attack on you. If you feel this way, it's time to stop, reflect, and center yourself. Remember, you and your child are on the same team.

Again, if you felt or said things initially that you now do not feel or wish you had not said, be kind to yourself. Forgive yourself. Have a follow-up conversation with your child if you need to, apologizing for anything untoward that may have come from your initial response. Children learn valuable lessons from adults taking responsibilities for their mistakes.

ATTACHMENT TO GENDER

When first becoming a parent, the prospect of one's child eventually becoming a different gender than originally thought is not usually within one's realm of conscious possibility. Parents begin planning, fantasizing, and formulating expectations for their child's life as soon as they're born; often as soon as they are conceived. Gender plays a big part in these expectations, which then have to shift a great deal when the gender expansiveness or different gender identity is revealed. This revelation comes as a shock to most parents, and it can be difficult to comprehend, particularly if the parents have not previously had experience with someone who is gender-diverse.

Also, there is typically an attachment to the gender of the child. When the child is in utero, most parents will say, "I don't care if it's a boy or a girl, as long as it's healthy." However, this thought often extends only until birth, when the sex of the baby (and supposed gender) is discovered. At that point, the parents assume the gender is static and will never change, and they therefore become invested in and begin "caring" about whether or not the baby is a boy or a girl.

It is harder, once attached to the child (and the gender you think they are), to stay in the place of focusing on health above all else. Remind yourself to be grateful for the life and health of your child, regardless of their gender expression or identity.

Of course, responses vary from one extreme to the other. Some parents get on board soon after hearing their child verbally reveal their true gender identity. Although rare, this can be because they've seen many signs of gender variance since early childhood, or sensed an unknown source of distress and see the relief the gender revelation brings. Other parents fight it and resist for a long while, struggling to have any type of acceptance. This is the more common response, likely because the parents have to shift ideas they had been formulating about their child's life since the child was born. There is also a distinct element of fear; fear they will "lose" their child, or that their child will become unfamiliar to them.

LOSS

Most, but not all, parents of transgender children experience some sense of loss. This is typically connected to thoughts of who they thought their child was, not who their child actually was.

Experiencing loss in relation to your child being transgender or transitioning is valid and something that deserves respect, acknowledgment, and time. While you are processing this and honoring this part of your journey, tenderly remind yourself you have not in fact lost your child. Your child is different than who you thought your child was. Your child is growing, expressing, individuating, and becoming authentic. Your child is not going away. Your child will be different to you, but not gone. Even while you are taking care of some difficult feelings associated with this adjustment, embrace and appreciate that your child is still here.

Some parents say the impending loss associated with transition feels like a death, and they prepare to grieve accordingly. Experiences will differ, but usually the fear and sadness surrounding the anticipation of feeling the loss of their child is likely stronger than the actual loss experienced. Again, focusing on the precious life of your child right in front of you can help temper these expected or actual feelings of loss.

YOUR FEELINGS ARE IMPORTANT

It's important you take care of yourself while taking care of your child. Having feelings of fear, dread, sadness, or loss doesn't make you bad; it makes you human. Working through these feelings is a part of the process. It is vital that you are able to support your child's gender identity with the unconditional love they absolutely need, no matter how old they are. The significance of the parent/child relationship is both what makes this difficult on you and why your acceptance is crucial to your child's happiness. Any feelings you have, particularly difficult ones, can prompt personal growth if you are open to it. Ask yourself, "How do I need to grow in order to truly and unconditionally love my child?"

Acknowledging all your feelings, including fear, is important when allowing your feelings to flow through you. Holding fear inside can prevent you from making conscious advancement. Alternatively, facing your fears can allow you to become more conscious. It can also better equip you with empowerment and energy. Acceptance will be a beautiful experience for you as well, as you will likely feel closer to your child when doing so. You will get to see them for who they really are, and they will likely trust you more for affirming them.

Ultimately, your acceptance will be one of the most important aspects on your child's journey. On this journey to acceptance and support, validate your feelings, be kind to yourself, find a place to be heard, and talk to other parents of transgender children. They are the people who can most relate to your rollercoaster of emotions on this path with your transgender child.

At first, some parents want to understand why their child is transgender. If you find yourself wondering the same thing, it may be helpful to remember that rarely do we search for the reason or cause of something unless it is seen as problematic. As being transgender is increasingly seen as simply a variation of the human condition, the impulse to figure out the "why?" will hopefully fade away. Additionally, more energy needs to be put toward advocacy, action, and acceptance, and the "why?" takes away from all of those things. Being transgender is not pathological, it just is something some people are. Just like any example of human diversity, some people are left-handed, and some people are not. Some people have two different-colored eyes, and some people don't. Some people are allergic to dairy, and some people are not. Some people are transgender, and some people are not.

Needs of the Transgender Child

The core need of the transgender child (and any child) is to feel as though they are okay any way they are. They need to be recognized for who they really are, and they probably need you to help get them to that place. Much like the needs of the gender-expansive child, your transgender child will need you to speak up for them, model acceptance, and pave the way during difficult situations.

Beyond that, the top need of your transgender child is to live fully and authentically. If your child is an assigned female who feels like a male, and is being addressed as a female and is considered a female, this is not living authentically. If your child is an assigned male who feels like a female, but is referred to with male pronouns and is categorized with boys in the home and classroom, this is not living authentically. This can cause great distress for your child and can prevent them from engaging fully in life. If your child is nonbinary but continues to be considered their assigned gender, or feels forced to "choose" a binary gender, this is not living authentically. In order to live authentically, the child needs to be given space to express their true self, and be affirmed when they do.

While being transgender is not a pathological condition like a "disease," it will be important for you to look at your child's being transgender as something concrete, like a medical condition. Your child will need you to weigh all the options in regard to how to best intervene in order to give them the best chance at a happy life.

Their Alignment; Your Transition

Often, there are two major aspects of discovering the transgender child's true gender identity: realizing they are transgender (the gender identity is something other than their sex at birth) and deciding *what to do about it*. To change one's previously considered gender to one that more closely reflects their brain gender identity is typically called *transition* ("change or passage from one state or stage to another"). However, the process a transgender person goes through is more like an *alignment*, and the process the loved ones go through is a transition. The transgender child is aligning themselves with their "real" gender. Transition is a way of making things right; it is not deciding to change something that is already right. The parents are the ones who have to fully transition from an idea they have about who their child is to something different. Although both parent and child are involved in this big change, these two perspectives can make this experience very different for each of you. This depends on whether you are aligning yourself with something that feels better to you, or having to transition to an idea that feels altogether foreign.

CHANGES

If your child undergoes social transition, they may begin using a different name and pronouns than those associated with their assigned gender at birth. This can be referred to as their "affirmed" name and pronouns, which is important: They are being affirmed for who they truly are. Most parents, particularly conscious parents, want to affirm their child; using the new name and pronouns is a very affirming thing to do.

Changing the name and pronouns for your child from something you have used the whole time you have known them can be hard and emotional. Some parents find themselves mourning the name, as they attached a lot of emotional meaning to it. They may find the pronouns much easier to change. Still others are the opposite, easily changing to a new name while struggling with the pronouns. Whatever your process, take care of yourself without your child knowing if it is hard on you. They are going through their own process and need attentive support from you. Make sure you are getting attentive support from someone else, as well.

Some children are quite impassioned when selecting their new name, and have had one in mind for a long time. While many parents are of the mindset that they should be able to choose their child's name, they often come to find their child already set on one. This is significant, and can be extremely empowering for your child. Yes, you likely named your child the first time around, but that was before they could communicate their own needs, motivations, and essence. Now that they are here, and now that they are their own unique being, allowing them to name themselves is a powerful and affirmative choice. If at first you don't particularly like the name they choose, sit with it. It will likely grow on you.

One of the most important aspects of making the name and/or pronoun switch is changing how you conceptualize your child. If you still see your child as their assigned gender at birth, switching to different pronouns will be difficult. If you work on embracing them and their essence as a different gender, the name and/or pronoun change will come much more naturally.

Important Points to Consider

Learning to detect when a child's gender expansiveness is indicative of the child being transgender is an important part of some parents' journey. Raising a transgender child can feel tricky at times, but in the end can be an incredibly enriching and powerful experience.

O Transgender and gender-expansive children will often present similarly when young, although there are important distinctions.

O Listen for your child to talk about who they are (identity), rather than just about what they want to do (expression).

O How strongly a child asserts their gender identity will depend upon temperament. Just because a child is not insistent upon having an alternate brain gender identity doesn't mean they don't.

O Transgender children will often say they have the hearts and brains of a gender that is different from their assigned gender at birth, or that they feel like a combination of genders. In some ways this could be an innocent acceptance of their concrete body (anatomy) and their abstract authentic gender experience (gender identity).

O Having a strong emotional response to having a transgender child is common. Reach out for support when necessary.

 **CHAPTER 7**

Trust Yourself

A conscious parent knows that the truth lies within. It does not come from external sources. Just as you desire your child to listen to their inner voice to become their authentic self, you must listen to your own inner voice so that you can be a conscious, authentic parent; one who is genuinely connected to your child and open to the wisdom they have to teach you. Know that throughout this gender journey, a grounded you is what your child really needs.

Listen to Your Gut

Parenting can be a test of your gut instincts. Not only *if* you have these instincts and how good they are but also how much you trust yourself to follow those instincts in the face of different outside influences, complex situations, and conflicting information. From the start, you get advice on how to raise your child: Everyone seems to have an opinion on where the baby should sleep, what the baby should wear, what the baby should eat, and so on. If you should encounter a challenge with your baby, everyone becomes an expert, and you may hear advice from others on what worked with *their* baby. Remember, your baby is different from anyone else's baby, and your baby needs parenting that is individualized based on their specific needs.

When complex situations arise, about anything, it is best to quiet the outside noise and center yourself to look within. When you are present with yourself, and slow down to allow answers to show themselves from within you, the situation may not seem as complex as it once did.

Such is true for the parent of a gender-expansive child. In addition to simply listening to your child, quelling complications from the outside will help your gut instincts to take over. If you are starting to feel that your child's gender expansiveness is a complex issue that is overwhelming you, come back to yourself. Remind yourself that you and your child both have the most authentic answers to whatever questions may arise along this journey.

YOUR RESPONSE CAN TEACH YOU

Pay attention to the feelings that arise in you when you see your child happy, particularly when it comes to feeling affirmed for their gender or gender expression. What is your gut telling you about this? Is it helping to guide you to the answers that will ultimately increase the frequency of your child's pure happiness? Additionally, pay attention to that "first response" feeling that arises in you if your child is distressed in regard to their gender or gender expression. That feeling will have the most valuable information for you. That is what your instincts are telling you to do, before other influences make you doubt yourself or complicate your thoughts. That gut feeling is the foundation you can build on, which is important to recognize before anxiety allows the worries to creep in and causes you to overanalyze.

Listen to your authentic voice. Listen to what your heart tells you. Do not stay in your head and intellectualize everything. Some of your feelings can't be intellectualized. Only when you are listening to your authentic voice can you hear your child's authentic voice, and encourage your child to do the same.

VISUALIZATION

If you can, make a recording of yourself reading the following visualization exercise and then listen to it when you are alone and comfortable. As you listen, close your eyes and let the words paint a picture for you.

> You are walking next to your child in a tall field of dried grass and weeds. You can feel the sun on your face, and smell the dusty, earthy scent of the field as the sun warms it as well. The wind blows gently, cooling your face and moving your hair. As the wind blows, you can hear the soft swishing of the weeds as they brush up against the weeds next to them. You sense your child moving next to you, but you are not speaking. You are in tune with their energy and their mood. Even as you walk in silence, not turning toward them, you are acutely aware of them.
>
> Without warning, a windstorm ensues. You tighten your leg muscles to brace yourself tighter against the earth. You close your eyes tightly to prevent particles of the weeds and grass from going into your eyes. Your arms and hands instinctually move to the sides of your face, lifting your collar to block your ears. You know your child is still there, next to you. Your child is okay. You are both in the chaos, but unafraid. You both know you need to wait until it is over, and it will be over soon. As suddenly as the windstorm began, it is over. All that was floating and tumbling in the air drops to the ground. The ensuing silence is almost

deafening. You feel as though you have been cleansed somehow, even if your physical body is dusty and disheveled. Keeping your eyes closed, you reach out for your child's hand. It is there, in an instant. Squeezing it tight, you turn toward your child and open your eyes. You see your child with a fresh perspective. Your child's energy and heart seem to appear from deep inside and you can see them glowing, bursting to come out. You remind yourself that you do know your child. You do know your child. Who is this child you so deeply know?

Stay Within Yourself

Part of being consciously aware means resisting the urge to be pulled in too many directions or to be influenced by too many factors. Stay within yourself and listen to yourself. Pare down extraneous factors or opinions that may be clouding your judgment. Especially during those situations that start to seem very complicated, take the time to be alone and quiet. This is when your true intentions are easily heard, and can take over the helm of your ship. Having respect for yourself and trusting yourself will help you to stay within your authentic self, and will help you resist the urge to constantly seek approval or advice from other sources. Respecting yourself can enhance the amount of love you can express toward yourself and others, particularly your child. Make wise, respectful decisions that reflect your personal beliefs. Showing respect toward yourself (and others) can increase your level of conscious awareness.

This aspect of your journey, staying within yourself, is in parallel with your child's process. Just as it is important for your child to stay within in order to know themselves fully and be their true self, it is important for you to stay within in order to be the most in tune, present parent you can be. Only when the two of you are grounded, and only when each of you are allowed to be your own authentic self, will the true potential for happiness come.

It's important to remember that the goal of a conscious parent is not to achieve perfection. Perfection is not possible. The goal of a conscious parent is to be aware of when you have moved from the conscious to the unconscious, and then be able to recenter yourself. Similarly, it's impossible to "stay within" 100 percent of the time. Inevitably, you will find yourself pulled in different directions, away from your true voice. If you are connected with yourself, you will be able to fairly quickly recognize when this is happening. When you find yourself moving away from yourself, come back. Recenter. Stay within. You can even say it out loud as you breathe: "Stay within. Stay within."

Trust Your Child

The next time you go looking for an expert, remember that you have one at home. You may need some assistance in deciding upon interventions or accessing resources, but in the area of their own gender identity your child knows best. Given a child's pure mind, you can rest assured they will have simpler answers than we adults do, and sometimes simple is exactly what you need. If your child is showing you or telling you what makes them feel happy, take it in as truth. Your child is closely connected to their authentic self because they have yet to develop the tendency to "overthink" things.

> Because your child wants to be seen for their authentic self, they will turn to those in charge of their care to help them be recognized in such a way. This is particularly true if their parent has shown themselves to be a source of safety and stability.

A confident, conscious approach to parenting will exhibit a deep trust in your child's ability to express their authentic self. This can be in relation to your child's gender identity, or in other areas. Consistently communicate that your child will be able to know themselves and express themselves as they are meant to. Your child will absorb this knowledge and will be able to more easily access their true self, even as they age. Your job as the parent is not to navigate the journey for them, but to provide gentle guidance for their own exploration.

This exploration can result in a number of different outcomes. Ultimately, your child can be confident in the knowledge that any way they are is okay, and that their authentic voice will be listened to. They may feel empowered to engage in authentic gender expression no matter what opposition they encounter in the outside world. This exploration may also result in your child understanding and asserting that they are not the gender they were assigned as at birth, and that they would like to be acknowledged as their true gender identity. This often involves social transition, which can feel more complicated for the parent than it does for the child. What greater practice is there in trusting your child than allowing them to transition? This is certainly a demonstration that you trust them enough to know their true gender identity and what they want to do about it.

WHAT IF THEY CHANGE THEIR MINDS?

If your child has expressed the need to transition, it's inevitable for parents to have some concerns and fears about this. Often this concern includes fears that their child may one day regret the transition or "change their mind" about being transgender. It's a valid concern, although fear of and concern about this happening seem to be incongruent with how frequently this happens.

When your child first presented with a gender identity that differed from their assigned gender, you may have found yourself hoping your child would change their mind. Even after you have walked through your initial responses and have come to realize this is your child's authentic self, your ongoing concern can turn into fear as transition nears or progresses.

Some of this fear and anxiety may come from trying to use your own perspective to understand. If you have never struggled with your gender identity, it's important that you try not to use your own perspective in this situation. If you try to imagine how you would feel if you transitioned to be acknowledged as a different gender, you might envision "changing your mind." This scenario is easily imagined because you are *not* transitioning to a gender that is authentically yours. As sure as you are about your gender identity, your transgender child is likely just as sure about theirs.

Projection is a part of parenting, just as it is for most relationships. The conscious parent will be aware (or will check in with themselves) about how they may be projecting their own perspective or feelings about transition onto their child.

STUDIES? STUDY YOUR CHILD

There are some outdated studies that show gender dysphoria in childhood doesn't usually persist. Keep in mind some of these studies were written by doctors who were actively trying to get the child to conform to their assigned gender at birth. Additionally, all the dynamics at play with the child's gender identity are not known in those studies. It will be interesting to see what kind of new research and statistics come from a more informed societal culture of affirming approaches to gender identity and expression. However, if you find yourself searching for research and statistics, you may be trying to intellectualize your child's gender journey. Try to move out of your head and into your gut, because this is where your most valuable information lies. If you trust yourself and your child, you will have less of a need for concrete numbers and research. Remind yourself no one knows your child like your child does. This is where to look for answers.

Most of the children, adolescents, and adults who say they are "sure" and then transition do not live to regret this decision. In fact, most report a much-improved satisfaction with life.

THE NONLINEAR PATH

Are there those who do change their minds about transitioning? Yes, there are. Just as they deserve support while finding their authentic selves during the initial transition, they deserve just as much support while listening to their authentic selves and transitioning back to their assigned gender at birth. Their gender may have evolved over time, or factors in their life may have influenced how they feel about their gender and transition. It is a very personal process, and it does not always follow a linear path.

Just because someone chooses not to transition, or later transitions back, does not mean they are not transgender. It means that they decided transitioning was ultimately not the best choice for them. It also does not mean that transitioning was not the best decision at that previous time in their life. For an individual who is in tune with their authentic being, transitioning and then later returning to present as and identify as their assigned gender at birth may be what they needed to do to reflect their most authentic self over the course of time. There do not seem to be detrimental outcomes for children who socially transition and then later decide they would like to be acknowledged as their assigned gender at birth. Most importantly, these children were shown they were listened to, they were respected, and their needs were responded to.

Of course, an important element when raising gender-expansive youth is that transition is not presented as the only option. When operating from a gender-affirming approach to parenting, you allow your child to explore and express themselves exactly as they are, without pressures to conform to society's standards or to fit in any particular "box." Your child should have the consistent communication that gender expression is personal and they are free to perform gender any way they would like, regardless of their assigned gender at birth. This will give them the freedom to be authentic in their expression without feeling like something has to change. However, being free to express or perform one's gender as they wish is not always enough. Some children will need to be recognized as their true gender identity in order to feel genuinely seen. It is important for a child to know all the options open to them in terms of exploring and expressing their gender identity.

There are no guarantees. If you are consciously aware of your longing for guarantees, accept this longing in a nonjudgmental way. Ask yourself if this is the best place to put your energy. If not, what can you do to redirect yourself to refocus on your child and their immediate needs? What other ways can you lower your anxiety about your child's gender journey?

Most things in life come with risks, but that does not mean that most things in life aren't worth doing. We as humans (probably as a self-protective measure) tend to look at the "worst-case scenarios" and feel scared by risks associated with choices, no matter how small those risks actually are. It's natural. However, this fear can scare us from taking the leap and prevent us from doing something we want to or need to do.

What if the ratio of successful airplane flights to the number of airplane crashes was roughly equivalent to the ratio of people who are satisfied about transitioning to those who regret it? If we all based our sense of safety on thinking about the small percentage of airplane crashes, none of us would want to fly again. While there is risk associated with flying, there are multiple benefits that come from it: seeing loved ones, seeing the world, adventure, business, and so on. With risk often comes adventure, new possibilities, fulfillment, and joy. Think of transitioning as your child spreading their wings to fly. If you find yourself getting caught up in fear, and the words "what if?" are starting most of your thoughts, regroup. Come back to yourself. Engage in the visualization exercise (in this chapter) again so you can be reminded that you do in fact know your child.

Model Mindfulness

Being mindful is being openly, actively in tune with the present moment. Unfettered by worries about the past or the future, the present can be the key to authenticity. This, in turn, helps you connect to yourself and your child. Of course, your mindfulness will be different from your child's, because mindfulness is a subjective experience of each moment. Realizing that mindfulness is subjective, and therefore uniquely yours, will help keep you from projecting your experience of the moment onto your child. Ultimately, the goal is for your child to witness you being mindful so that they can feel able to be mindful themselves. A child who is frequently contending with the projections of a parent does not learn how to quiet their own mind in order to connect with their inner compass.

Mindfulness can be modeled both implicitly and explicitly. As you know, your child watches you for cues on how to handle stress, the reactions of other people, and intense feelings. Model deep breaths: Have your child observe you stopping in the moment and taking a deep breath to recenter yourself. Verbalize using techniques that help quiet the mind and body: "Right now I'm relaxing my muscles so my body is not so tense, and I can think more clearly" or "I'm telling my worries to be still so I can hear what my heart is telling me." Also, verbalize conscious thought processes and decision-making techniques, such as: "My heart is telling me to . . . ," "The idea I keep coming back to is . . . ," or "I need to sit with this and quiet my mind so the answer will be more clear to me." Ask questions that encourage mindfulness, such as: "What is your heart telling you?" or "If you can turn off your worries, what do you hear?" Gently guiding your child to a state of mindfulness can help them be more authentically in tune with their gender identity.

Your child's thought process will inevitably be influenced by peers and the outside world. For this reason it's important that you model for your child how to "stay within" and come back to themselves for the true answers about their authentic self. This ability will serve them well throughout childhood, into adolescence, and adulthood.

MINDFULNESS MANTRAS

Having mindfulness mantras (like the following) at your fingertips can help you remember the space you'd like to be in. Additionally, reminding yourself that mindfulness is a choice can be a powerful tool to keep yourself on the right path.

O I choose to stay within.

O I choose to listen to my inner compass.

O I choose to quiet the worries.

O I choose to accept my emotions and thoughts as they come and go.

O I choose to trust myself when others may doubt.

○ I choose to see my child and their true self.

○ I choose to move forward as my child leads me.

Important Points to Consider

It can be hard to trust yourself and your child when you are very worried about others' opinions. Set yourself free from obligations to please everyone and tune in instead to your inner voice and the inner voice of your child. Staying mindful will help you accomplish this and will likely help you enjoy the journey a bit more with your child.

○ The truth lies within, both within yourself and within your child. When you are consciously aware, these truths are more readily seen.

○ Let your gut guide you. Your gut responses are most authentic, and will lead you to the best choices regarding your child.

○ Using visualizations can help you metaphorically grasp important concepts about the essence of your child rather than focusing too much on extraneous factors.

○ Staying within yourself will help you minimize outside distractions and complications that may cloud your ability to most clearly see where your child is on their gender journey.

○ Being a conscious parent will help you to confidently trust your child to explore their own gender and authentically share with you who they truly are. Trusting your child helps you embrace risk as you pursue their happiness, without fear of regret taking over.

○ Being mindful will help you engage with the present moment, which is where authenticity and happiness live. Being mindful will not only help you stay connected to your child, but you will also teach your child this most essential skill.

 **CHAPTER 8**

Stay in the Now

Your right now is this very moment. Your now is your most precious asset, because in the scheme of things it's all you have. Knowing how to stay in the now can help you appreciate the one thing that is truly yours: this moment. Stress, fear, regret, and other distractions that take you away from being conscious are the very things that rob you of your now. This chapter will discuss how you can honor the past without living in it, avoid borrowing trouble from the future, and get the most out of your present moments.

The Present

Your place of power is always in the present moment. Staying in the present moment allows you to minimize negative feelings that may be lurking when you think about the past or future. It's important to be consciously aware of your thoughts and possible motivations for thinking them so that you can build an understanding of your here and now. When you fully understand your here and now, you can connect with the many possibilities available to you.

Particularly with a gender-expansive child, worries and thoughts about the past and future can be frequent if you don't consciously try to stay within the present moment. That is not to say there will not be thoughts about the past or the future; it simply means your emotions should not be ruled by these thoughts.

Especially when feeling high emotions, remember that the present is your place of groundedness. Staying conscious allows you to accept the things you can't change, rather than to resist or fight things over which you have no power. Staying in your own skin allows you to remain steady when things around you are uncertain or start to change.

In this fast-paced world, it's difficult to slow down and silence the diversions that keep you from being mindful. However, it's essential that you do slow down and live in the moment so that you can be the wisest version of yourself. It is only then you will be able to attend to your inner compass, just as you want your child to be able to do with theirs.

It will be hard for you to be a conscious parent when you are stressed. Your job is to manage your stress in general, which in turn will positively affect your ability to stay grounded in the present. This includes engaging in basic self-care of both body and mind. It involves being aware of your thoughts and feelings as they arise, without letting them control you. It allows you to observe your child's personal needs, without projecting your own feelings and expectations on them. Additionally, attuning to your child in the present moment allows you to listen to them with a more mindful perspective than if you are being swallowed up by past regrets or future concerns.

It's important to remember that the present is where your child actually lives. The child you have, the one in front of you, lives in the present and is here now.

Complicating thoughts about who your child was in the past or may be in the future can cause you to lose sight of your present-day child. In doing so, you might miss out on the joy, wisdom, and gifts your child has to offer, today. Is there something you can do that can help you embrace your child in the moment? If worries about their gender journey are clouding your ability to enjoy the now, can you create some genderless moments? For example, have moments when you commit to celebrate the present with your child, no matter what they choose to wear, play with, or act. What might you be missing in the everyday moments with your child if you are too focused on those things?

Children have a much more innate sense of how to stay in the present than adults do. Let your child guide you. If you see your child being authentic and genuine in the moment, join them. Try to view the moment from their perspective. You might be surprised at what you see. Conversely, if you see your child struggling with sadness or anxiety, bringing yourself back to the present moment will help them to do the same. Sadness or anxiety is likely tied to points of time outside of the present moment.

MINDFUL MOMENTS

A mindfulness technique that you can teach your child—and utilize yourself—involves using your senses to ground yourself in the present moment. You can use this technique anywhere you are, and you can do this without any preparation. The following technique asks you to engage all of your senses, and can help you feel a considerable difference in your muscle tension and stress. If you want, record yourself reading the following meditation aloud so that you can play it back with your eyes closed.

- O Sit down. Pause. Relax your muscles, particularly your shoulders, so you feel yourself melt a little more into the place you are sitting. Feel the seat underneath you, where your body makes contact with it. Place your hands on the seat and move them back and forth to take note of the texture of the seat. Focus only on that as you take a deep breath.

- O Notice the temperature of the room. Can you feel the temperature of the air on your face? Is it cool, warm, or almost entirely neutral? Focus only on that as you take a deep breath.

- O Check into the sounds that are present in the room with you. Perhaps the hum of a machine, the ticking of a clock, sounds of life around you? Can you hear any sounds of nature? Focus only on that as you take a deep breath.

- O As you breathe, do you notice any scents? Are there any subtle scents in your surroundings you had not noticed before? Focus only on that as you take a deep breath.

- O Look around you. What do you see? What colors do you notice? What shapes? Is there movement, or only still objects? Focus only on that as you take a deep breath.

If needed, run through this exercise one more time.

The Past Has Its Place

The past is typically a poignant place for parents. You can probably remember when you first learned the news that your child was joining your family. Loving and intentional preparations were made to create a place in your family for this child. Many of these preparations were likely influenced by gender assumptions, such as the colors you picked for your child's nursery, the clothing you selected, and how you selected your child's name. You may have many memories of your child as a baby and toddler, dressed in gendered clothing. No doubt some of the memories have heavily influenced what you thought your child's gender was.

> The memories of your child's past are yours, and they are important. Your child's transition does not mean the past is being cancelled out; it simply means the past takes on new meaning. Your child may have a different relationship with the past than you do, and that's okay. Let your relationship with the past be what it needs to be, as long as it feels healthy to you.

The past may carry with it reminders of previous points on your child's gender journey. You may yearn for the past, before you knew your child's gender identity was something other than their assigned gender at birth. You may recall times when you were less involved in your understanding of gender, and they carry with it painful memories of how you used to try to control or manage your child's gender expression. You may look back and see "signs" that your child did not identify as their assigned gender, and you may have feelings associated with how you responded to those signs.

A SENSE OF GRIEF

When parents of a transgender child experience feelings of grief and loss, these feelings are typically associated with the past. The past has its place in your journey to acceptance. However, the past should be seen as a place to briefly visit, and is certainly not a place to live.

If you feel the need to grieve, allow these feelings to come. Invite them in without judgment. This may be part of your healing process. Allow yourself to grieve for the ideas you had about your child's gender, and what that meant to you.

This may be a time to gently remind yourself that your child has always been their own person, not an extension of you but their own unique being. The ideas you had about their gender were your own, and may not have been the reality of your child's experience. Let yourself release these ideas, without interpreting this letting go as having to let go of your child.

The antidote for experiencing grief and loss in regard to your transgender child is connecting with your child in the here and now. Doing so will remind you that your child is still here; that this beautiful human being you brought into existence is still on this amazing journey of life. Not your journey, but their own journey. This is a journey for you to witness and behold, only offering gentle guidance when necessary.

The more you are intimately in tune with your child's essence, the more you will feel you have the same child in the present as you did in the past. When you are in tune, you will likely experience fewer feelings of grief and longing, because your "past" child will seem more authentically connected with your present child.

If you find yourself consistently visiting the past to the point that it is disrupting your present moment, consider engaging in some exercises to help you let go. These may include writing a letter to the past and explaining why you need to set it free. Or, create something that represents your child in the present, and focus your energy on that. Engage in mindfulness techniques to bring yourself back to the present.

Worry/Fear for the Future

Fear and anxiety are typically associated with concerns about the future. Sometimes these worries and concerns are not associated with concrete or even probable outcomes. They are usually more associated with projections of your current feelings onto the future. These projections can make the future seem like an unstable and scary place. Often when you don't know the future, you "fill in the blank" with ideas about potential outcomes. These may be rational/irrational or probable/improbable, but they can feel so real that you can get very closely connected with them to the point where they may feel like they have already happened. Being consciously aware of these projections and fears is the key to understanding how real they feel in the present.

Unless your safety is being threatened in the present moment, fear and anxiety have no place. The present moment will bring with it opportunities to do all sorts of wonderful things: connect, problem-solve, attune, address, enjoy. Don't miss out on these opportunities by being lost in the past. Some present moments bring with them their own negative emotions and challenges. When you stay in the present moment, these challenges are more manageable. Your life leading up to your future is a series of present moments, which are more manageable when you take one present moment at a time.

BORROWING TROUBLE

If you are experiencing joys and challenges in the present, and then you also take a worry from the future and invite it into your present moment, this is called "borrowing trouble." Certainly life can be complicated enough without creating anxiety-provoking scenarios in your head that disrupt your state of mind in the here and now.

Minimizing your thoughts about the future is not to say that you won't have challenges, but you rarely have any power over those future moments in the present. Your energy is wasted by worrying about something that has not yet presented itself or may never present itself.

If you find yourself borrowing trouble, let that serve as a sign that you need to bring yourself back to the present. Where is your power right now? What feelings are associated with your right now? What positive feelings or experiences might you be missing because you are focusing on a place that is not yet here?

Getting the Most Out of the Now

If the now is where your energy is best spent, then how do you make the most of it? Watching for your child's joy and happiness, as well as your own, is a good place to start. There are almost always good things happening around you if you stop to look for them.

Additionally, being open-minded can help you get the most out of the now and become a more conscious person. If you have rigid ideas and expectations of how things "should" be, you will miss out on many positive things about the way things are. Accept the diversity of life, and embrace the unexpected aspects of this life you have. If you become resistant to changes or things that are outside of your expectations, you enter into a lower level of conscious awareness.

FLUCTUATIONS OF JOY

Children are, by nature, typically very joyful beings. Your child's gender expansiveness, if not met with affirmation, may have been a source of distress for them. If your child was dysphoric because of an authentic gender identity that differed from their assigned gender, you may not have seen a lot of uninhibited joy from your child. Addressing and affirming their gender expression or identity will hopefully unleash the natural joy inherent within your child.

Ironically, at the same time parents experience the increasing joy that comes from affirming their child, they may themselves struggle with their own feelings about their child and who they thought their child was. Parents may have had a lot of expectations tied up with gender, all of which seem to be shifting. Your joy may feel as though it's been stifled a little bit, even as your child's joy is expanding. While you may need to give yourself some time to adjust, being conscious can help make this journey easier.

If you are very connected to your child, you can experience joy as they are experiencing it. You will recognize that your child is not an extension of yourself, but their own unique, beautiful being. When you relinquish ownership of your child and especially your child's gender, you are free to simply enjoy things as they are. If you find yourself temporarily unable to do this, remind yourself that these feelings are transient. Allow them to sit with you while being acknowledged. However, you may need to eventually excuse yourself from these feelings so that you can go and join in with your child (and their joy) exactly as they are.

> During all the stages of your child's gender journey, there is happiness to be had. Happiness is genderless. Staying consciously connected to your child in the present moment will help you embrace those moments of happiness that are yours for the taking.

GRATITUDE

Gratitude is a sentiment that is very closely connected with one's present moment. Gratitude is typically based upon the gifts and opportunities that are available to you in the present. Gratitude and sadness don't coexist well, nor do gratitude and anxiety. It is difficult to be sad and anxious when you are grateful for something. Even if aspects of your child's gender expansiveness have been difficult for you, they have the potential to have a positive impact on you. Your ability to appreciate this will allow you to reach higher levels of consciousness.

No matter where you or your child is in relation to the gender journey, there are things to be grateful for. What have your unique gifts been along this journey? What has it opened up in you? Some examples of gratitude could include:

○ Grateful your child is here.

○ Grateful that your child is connected enough with you to either show you or tell you about their authentic gender experience.

- Grateful for other people in your child's life who are gender affirming.

- Grateful for resources available to you to help support your child.

- Grateful for your own understanding of why being a conscious parent is important and how it can help both of you on this journey.

- Grateful for the many strengths inherent in both you and your child.

- Grateful for your own ability to embrace the many possibilities of gender and see how intricate it is.

- Grateful for a community you may not otherwise have known.

Take the time to write your own list of gratitude. Being aware of all you have to be grateful for helps you be more present and happier in the now.

Life is full of gifts that don't appear to be gifts at first. When your heart is open to the unique experience of life, you can realize what gifts have been given to you. Even your child's gender journey, which may have seemed overwhelming at first, may end up feeling like a gift to be grateful for. Use this insight as a reminder that there are gifts in your life that have yet to be seen.

Focus on Small Goals

If you find yourself too closely connected with the past or the future, and if coming back to the present seems overwhelming to you, come up with small goals you can focus on. These goals can also help you prioritize if you feel you have gotten off-track from what is most important to you. Setting positive goals and working to accomplish them can help you become more consciously aware.

While to-do lists certainly have their place, focusing solely on completing tasks can keep you in your head. Completing tasks and crossing off items on a to-do list is an intellectual task. In order to connect yourself more fully with your emotional self, make goals that revolve around self-care and mindfulness. Some examples could be:

- O Engage in a self-care activity

- O Complete a visualization exercise

- O Make a gratitude list

- O Engage in a creative activity, preferably with your child

- O Create a parenting, family, or household mission statement

- O Give your child undivided attention for twenty minutes, either playing with them or having a conversation with them

Notice that most of these goals have to do with the present moment. Even creating the mission statement, while it could positively affect the future, prompts you to make choices in the moment that are in line with your parenting priorities.

Important Points to Consider

While at first you may find yourself thinking a lot about the past, staying conscious will help you to enjoy the present. It is in the present where you have the most ability to experience your child as they genuinely are. The future is something that is yet to be known, so worrying about it is a distraction from the present and a drain on your energy resources. Stay in the now in order to maximize your potential for happiness.

- O Sadness and anxiety live in the past and future, clouding your ability to embrace the gifts of the present.

- O Techniques that help you stay in the present include slowing down, being grateful, and accepting the things you can't change.

- O You have the most power over your ability to be happy and authentic in the present moment.

O Focusing on your child today will help lovingly anchor you to the here and now.

O While the past can be visited in regard to your gender-expansive child, joy may not be as present there as it is in the now. Return to the present for your own joy and to witness the joy of your child. There are many opportunities for happiness all along the gender journey.

CHAPTER 9

Interventions

There are a number of different interventions possible on the journey of a gender-expansive child. Some interventions may not feel like you are doing much except observing, listening, and affirming. Nonetheless, these are very powerful interventions for your gender-expansive child. Other interventions have more to do with external influences in the form of advocacy. Transition is an intervention that is only appropriate for transgender children. Transitioning is something one does if one's gender identity doesn't match their assigned gender at birth, and you as the parent will likely need to help facilitate this if necessary.

Observe and Affirm

Does your child's gender expansiveness indicate they have a gender identity other than what is congruent with their assigned sex? Perhaps. Or maybe your child's gender expansiveness is simply that, a demonstration that gender itself is personal, wide-ranging, and multidimensional.

Once we as a society can let go of the rigid expectations of gender, some children won't be seen as "gender nonconforming" anymore. They will simply be seen as children. Children, like adults, have endless possible combinations of personality types, interests, and ways of being.

If your child is simply expressing interest in things that are typically associated with another gender, there is nothing you need to do except affirm their choices, allow them to be themselves, and communicate "Any way you are is okay" both verbally and nonverbally. The only other thing to do at this point is to observe your child on their gender journey.

WATCH FOR DISTRESS

Taking an affirmative approach is about allowing your child to just be. If you are engaging in this practice and your child is still not happy, try to assess where the unhappiness is stemming from. If your child is showing signs of distress, try to discern the triggers and underlying causes. Is your child feeling free to express themselves as they wish, without concern about what others will think, or what you will think? Are they feeling constrained to hide how they think and feel, how they would really prefer to dress and play? Are they feeling shameful about their interest or their natural inclinations? If yes, your child may be experiencing inner turmoil, which results in distress. Sometimes that distress can manifest itself in somatic symptoms such as stomachaches or headaches. Other times a child can externalize their distress in behavioral acting out. Some children begin to have mood dysregulation, becoming emotional at the drop of a hat. You may see an increase in anxious or depressive symptoms. If the distress persists, this may be an indication of underlying feelings about their gender expansiveness or gender dysphoria.

Listen to your child. Affirm your child. Watch for signs of distress. If changing the acceptance of your child's natural inclinations or gender expression seems to alleviate your child's distress, you're on the right track. You do not need to do anything at this time except communicate love and acceptance, and make sure that the other environments your child is in do the same.

If your child is not policed on their gender expression, and your child is happy, continue engaging in informed listening and open communication. You can ask questions about their gender identity to make sure your child knows they can communicate about this with you, but there is no urgent need to act. It's important to educate gender-expansive children on the wide variety of gender identities that exist, and have conversations about how everyone has their own unique gender identity. The concept of nonbinary identities is relatively abstract, and because children operate on a concrete level they will have difficulty articulating it. Simply help your child understand that everything is on a spectrum, and that they don't have to "pick" one gender or the other.

Advocate

As many of you reading this book likely already know, as a parent you are going to have to advocate for your gender-expansive child. You may need to speak up and ask for things your child wants, especially if your child is not able to speak up for themselves yet. You will also need to advocate in other environments where your child spends time, such as school, daycare, church, camp, friends' houses, and so on. You may need to remind yourself that your top priority is your child's happiness. Making other people in other environments feel comfortable is not your primary concern.

Advocating for your child about what your child wants and needs will model the concept for them so that they can learn how to do it themselves. Additionally, your child learns that they can count on you and that you are speaking up for them without judgment.

Your advocacy will not only serve to change things for your child, but you will be changing the world for other children as well. Each parent who advocates for a more open view of gender is changing society, a little bit at a time.

If your child does transition, in any sense of the word, you will likely need to advocate for their rights in a variety of situations and settings. Many parents are afraid of being accused of "leading" their child when it comes to gender identity and interventions, including transition. These accusations often come from people who do not fully understand gender identity. Gender identity cannot be created by an outside source; it is something intrinsic in all of us. Once a parent understands the true gender identity of their child, they may find themselves in the tricky position of advocating for their child to be able to transition. Naysayers may point fingers at the parent, implying the parent is acting on their own ideas and desires rather than those of the child. However, it is every parent's task to intervene on behalf of their child when they see that something is needed for their child's health and well-being.

Living Life Fully: The Oxygen Example

If you are like most people, you haven't had to think much about your lungs. You were born with fully functioning lungs that have faithfully delivered oxygen to your body and brain, just as they are supposed to. You can't imagine it any other way, simply because it's never been any other way for you. You've also probably not given much thought to the role oxygen plays in your life, because it's always been there; as much as you need, delivered when you need it, without complication. For anyone who's briefly experienced a decrease in oxygen, or lack of oxygen, that person will likely never forget the feeling of panic and the intense, primal need to have oxygen fill the lungs once again.

Now, picture this: You were born with something wrong with your lungs; they can't fully absorb and process oxygen the way that most people's lungs can. You can take in just enough oxygen to live, but you cannot get enough to fully engage in life. Since you were born with your lungs not doing precisely what they should do, you spend every day of your life not being able to do all the things you would otherwise like to do. You spend many of your days wishing your lungs were different, wishing you could breathe as fully and deeply as everyone around you. You watch everyone take those deep, life-sustaining breaths, and you can tell that none of them realize how lucky they are; their lungs (and the resulting oxygen they get) are simply taken for granted. You stand there, taking shallow, ragged breaths, feeling weak and somewhat listless.

Then one day, you stumble across something on the Internet: Sub-Par Oxygenation Syndrome.* (*Not a real syndrome.) You discover there is a name for what you've been experiencing, and you discover that other people have it, too. You feel relieved, validated, and excited. Then you read about an intervention that is available for this syndrome. While it may not give you new lungs, there is a machine that can deliver this life-enhancing oxygen straight to you: an oxygen tank. It's expensive (insurance doesn't cover it in this scenario), but you know you'll do anything to get access to one.

The day you get your oxygen tank feels like the most liberating, exciting day of your life. You put it right on (it comes in a nifty backpack), and then you put the tubes under your nose. To breathe so fully and so easily is something you've longed for your whole life, but never thought you'd experience. (At times, you feel sad and resentful that you have to wear such a contraption to feel the way most others were born feeling, but you continue to be grateful nonetheless.)

When you explain to those close to you what you've discovered and show them your new oxygen tank, they're skeptical: "Really? Are you sure you're not getting enough oxygen? I get plenty of oxygen every time I take a deep breath. Perhaps you're not doing it right." Others don't like your oxygen tank: "Hmmm, I liked you better before you wore that tank. I'm not used to seeing you with those tubes. Can you please take it off?"

You're saddened and shaken by these responses, but you don't take it off. The oxygen tank brings you too much relief and too much life to give it up.

SOMETHING REAL

While being transgender is not a disability, gender dysphoria is something real, much in the same way that not getting enough air is real. The irony of the oxygen tank example is that if someone had been born with lungs that didn't deliver enough oxygen, it would likely have been caught right away by medical doctors. An intervention would have been offered early on, and the doctors would have recommended it with confidence. Treating gender variance is a bit trickier; a person's need for their gender identity to be validated is not as immediately evident as one's need for adequate oxygen would be. While we still have a long way to go, intervening with children who communicate a persistent "other" gender identity is much like offering the oxygen tank to the person who needs it: "I know what you need; here you go."

Don't wait for your child to manifest problem behaviors, insist that they are transgender, or ask to transition in order to open up the lines of communication. Ask a lot of questions about how your child is feeling. If you sense gender is a source of internal conflict or stress for your child, make it known that this topic is welcomed in your home.

Ask creative questions to find out how your child experiences their gender. Be honest about options that are available in regard to transitioning. (Doing so will not make your child transgender or "plant" ideas in their head. Transition is not an appealing option for a child who is not transgender.) If you still sense that your child is in distress but they are not being open about their feelings, seek a consultation with a gender therapist trained in interviewing children. The benefits of early intervention—and transition, if right for the child—are many.

Finding the Right Gender Therapist

Finding a good gender therapist for your child can be a daunting task. If someone claims to be a gender "expert," don't assume your hunt is over. Ask questions (see the following list for sample questions) and always go with your gut instincts. Ultimately, *you* are the expert on your child, and *your child* is the expert on their gender.

SAMPLE QUESTIONS FOR A POTENTIAL GENDER THERAPIST

- How long have you worked with children?
- Have you been trained interviewing children in a non-leading manner?
- How involved are the parent(s) in the assessment/therapy with the child?
- What is your opinion about how young a child can understand their gender identity?
- What is your general opinion on letting a child express their own gender identity?

And, depending upon where your child is in their gender journey:

- What are your thoughts on social/medical transition for transgender youth?

After you have met with the therapist two or three times, re-evaluate how the sessions are going for both you and your child. Is your child comfortable? Are you? If not, address your concerns with the therapist. The therapist should be open to your feedback and be able to explain their reasoning behind the treatment methods. If things don't change, begin your search again.

If the therapist seems to focus on changing your child or getting your child to conform to the gender roles associated with their assigned gender at birth, do not hesitate to terminate immediately. This is known as "reparative" or "conversion" therapy and is illegal in some states. There is plenty of evidence that shows this method of treatment is extremely damaging to the children who are subjected to it.

If you are struggling to find a gender therapist who is right for your family, reach out for help online. There are several groups that can help you find one in your area (see Appendix E).

STRUCTURE OF SESSIONS

There is no exact science to how a gender therapist might structure sessions, but in general there should be a good balance of meeting with you and meeting with your child. The therapist should meet alone with you as part of the assessment process and at other times as needed throughout treatment. This is because you need to have free reign to say what you want to say about your child's gender expression and your feelings about it. Your child should not hear all of your thoughts, opinions, and feelings about their gender expression or identity. Children tend to try to take care of their parents and avoid causing their parents distress. Therefore, hearing statements made by parents (particularly those expressing resistance) can impact the child's ability to say what they want and need in regard to gender expression, identity, transitioning, and so on. This can have serious ramifications on their mental health and future.

Similarly, your child should have the opportunity to speak alone with the gender therapist so that they may speak their mind without censoring things out of regard for their parents. The gender therapist will not tell you exactly what your child has said while in private, but when you are all together the therapist should help your child communicate better with you. To better facilitate communication among all participants, joint sessions are also called for when it comes to working with youth. It is important for family members to learn how to talk to one another about gender, and to become more comfortable with the topic. Additionally, parents tend to be better historians and reporters of behaviors, which can be extremely beneficial to the treatment course.

LET YOUR CHILD LEAD

As with any therapy, or reason for seeking therapy, the gender therapist should not enter into therapeutic work with you and your family with an agenda. Ultimately, the child sets the agenda based on their needs and clinical presentation. If you get the sense that the therapist has their mind set on accomplishing something specific (such as getting your child to transition or not transition), consider that to be a red flag.

Every child and family is different, each with their own unique story and needs. Some of the interventions and suggestions will be similar to those used with other families, but most will be tailor-made to your family and what is specifically going on with your child at that point in time.

> Your child will be the best source of information regarding their gender identity. Children of a very young age are aware of what gender they are, and/or what gender expression they are comfortable with.

Although your child leads the way, you play an essential role on this journey. You will be an excellent historian for how your child has expressed their gender from an early age, their current significant behaviors, any signs of distress, and so on. Of course, part of the gender therapist's job will be to work with you in regard to your feelings about your child's gender expansiveness, and your feelings about potential options for your child's future.

RED HERRINGS

Many parents are witness to their child's gender expansiveness *and* a lot of other emotions and behaviors. Sometimes it can be hard to tell which emotions and behaviors are elicited by authentic gender struggles. Those emotions and behaviors that seem unrelated to gender identity but may actually be symptoms of the distress caused by dysphoria or nonconformity can be considered "red herrings." The gender therapist can help you sift through some of these factors to find out what needs to be addressed first.

It is common for some extraneous emotions and behaviors to be resolved once the gender expression is affirmed or the gender identity is validated. One good way to narrow down what is really going on with your child is to focus on what seems to be causing them the most distress.

For example, if your child is having problems with social skills or academics, and they are showing signs of a gender identity that does not match their body, they might have anger outbursts and exhibit anxiety. Step back and think about these things. What seems to bring your child the most mental distress? What do they talk about the most? What seems to trigger misbehavior or alter their mood the most? What do they shed the most tears over? Answers to these questions will help show you what needs to be addressed first.

Concern about anger outbursts and academic problems are what typically bring parents the most distress, and therefore this is what most parents want addressed first. This may be like putting a bandage on an injury without treating the cause, or it might mean the child spends too much time addressing something that is not causing them the most pain or distress. Parents may feel like gender is something that can wait until the other more urgent issues are addressed, but sometimes the child cannot have any resolution in the other areas until gender is addressed.

In some cases, it will be the therapist's job to gently prevent you from following the red herrings. Conversely, if your child's therapist seems determined to only focus on these red herrings and not address the gender topic, this should also be a red flag for you. While you may feel some relief if the gender therapist recommends holding off on making any major decisions or wants to address everything else other than the gender identity, pay attention to what your gut is telling you. You know your child. If the therapist's recommendations seem to bring your child more distress, something has gone awry. If the therapist's recommendations seem to bring a happier, more relaxed child with fewer externalizing behaviors, they are on the right track.

On Being "Sure"

When parents intervene on behalf of their child, especially in regard to major decisions, they want to be "sure." They want to have all the information possible to help them make choices, and they often want quantifiable data in order to support the intervention they are choosing for their child. Because there are not a lot of concrete factors when it comes to "knowing" if one's child is transgender (and therefore in need of transition), parents instead need to rely on the relatively abstract concept of their child's self-report of gender identity. This can feel a little risky, and many parents find themselves looking for ways to figure out if their child is sure this is the right thing for them.

One's gender identity (something that is) and the act of transitioning (something one does) are two separate entities. From the standpoint that one is born with an innate gender identity, being transgender is not a "decision." Transition often means acting upon something that already is.

Parents can get caught up in the concept of allowing a young child to make a major decision about their lives, when they wouldn't allow the child to make big decisions about most other things. If you can recenter yourself to the fact that your child's gender identity is something that already is, allowing your child to transition will start to seem less like a big, heavy decision and more like a natural intervention.

Some parents express concerns that their child may not be "able" to know their gender enough to guide what to do about it. If your child is of sound judgment and mind, and rooted to reality (and they likely are), there is no reason to believe they don't have the ability to know their gender or know what they'd like to do about it. Having a mood disorder or mental illness does not preclude one's ability to understand their gender. These things may confound coping with gender incongruence or transition, but they do not undermine a child's ability to know their gender identity.

THE PURITY OF A YOUNG MIND

One beautiful aspect of being able to see the pure gender identity and desires of transgender youth is that (unlike adults) their brains have not yet been trained to focus on everything that could go wrong with any given scenario. Unless there are other complicating factors, a young person's gender identity and what they would like to do about it are relatively simple. Because children don't overthink things, being transgender and transitioning are often fluidly connected. Remain mindful and stay connected to your child; this will help you avoid "overthinking" matters as your adult brain wants you to do.

We are so used to warning our children of possible outcomes that we forget some outcomes are natural consequences to a needed intervention, not something to avoid at all costs. Will there possibly be difficult times ahead for the transgender child who opts to transition? Yes. Will you be there to help them through it? Yes.

If your child had a medical condition, and a doctor recommended an intervention that could make their lives better, or potentially even save your child's life, you would not ask your child to "make the decision" about the intervention. Indeed, you would try to make the decision based on the information in front of you. Would you present the options to your child but then warn them to consider the financial implications, social implications, and family implications on said intervention? Likely not.

Given how debilitating and dangerous dysphoria can be, any stumbling blocks post-transition will likely be easier to overcome than the distress of not transitioning at all.

Transition Options

Just as there is a wide range of gender identities, there are many different options and interventions for the gender-expansive child. "Transition" can mean many different things, and can look many different ways. The main goal of transition (no matter what that may look like) is to help your child feel understood and honored for their authentic self, and to alleviate any existing dysphoria if possible. Transition can be custom-made to the individual, on the gender binary or not, including but not limited to the following examples:

- Social transition only
- Changing name and pronouns
- Changing pronouns only
- Changing name only
- Social and medical transition
- Changing certain elements of gender expression
- Legal name and gender change

If the transition involves changing pronouns, the new pronouns should best reflect the true gender identity. If your child's gender identity is nonbinary or genderqueer, they may choose to use gender-neutral pronouns such as "they/them/theirs." Some people struggle with the concept of the "singular they," but this pronoun has been around for centuries, and it is used more often than you might think. You likely use a singular they to describe someone when gender does not play a part in the conversation, i.e., "They dropped it off on the porch" or "They said they would file the paperwork in the morning." It might take some time, but you will get used to using it for your child. Remember that the most important part of this pronoun change is that your child is feeling acknowledged for who they really are.

Social Transition

For a young transgender child, an appropriate intervention may include social transition. This involves different things depending on the child and how they were presenting prior to transition. Social transition typically includes changing appearances (such as hairstyle or way of dressing) so that one is "read" as their true gender when out in public. Social transition also often involves changing pronouns to reflect the child's gender identity (options include but are not limited to he/him/his, she/her/hers, and they/them/theirs). Frequently, social transition includes a name change. Some young children opt to keep their birth names, particularly if the name is gender-neutral. The older a child is, the more inclined they may be to change their name (even a gender-neutral one) due to the personal association it may have to their assigned gender at birth.

Many people are perplexed about the concept of a child making a big "decision" such as transitioning. One thing to remember is that gender identity is not a decision. It is a way one is. For children who have shown a persistent and consistent gender identification during childhood, who express a strong desire to be seen as the gender with which their brain identifies, and who show distress when they are not, then transition is an intervention to help them be who they truly are.

No medical interventions happen at the initial stage of social transition, particularly for a prepubescent child. When a child has been clear about their gender identity and it seems that prolonging transition is causing distress, transitioning young can be incredibly beneficial to the individual.

The best way to reduce suffering of children who are struggling with dysphoria is to allow them to be seen for who they truly are. This may include allowing them to transition, or live on the "spectrum," which may be outside the gender binary. Living authentically is a basic human right for all people.

An interesting aspect of social transition often includes a fairly binary way of expressing gender, even for the child who may naturally be more fluid in gender expression. For the child who wants to be seen as male in society, they may choose to express themselves in a very masculine way at first. For the child who wants to assert themselves as female, they may express themselves in a very feminine way at first. This allows others to use concrete cues to get used to the affirmed gender, and to get used to using new pronouns. Likewise, strong binary expressions of gender allow the child to feel more confident that they will be read as their true gender when out and about. Once they have socially transitioned and feel more confident that others see them as their "true" gender, they can begin to allow themselves to express their gender in a more fluid way and not restrict themselves to things society has deemed masculine or feminine. However, some children do not allow themselves to relax into their true way of gender expression until after medical transition.

TRANSITION FOR THE NONBINARY CHILD

Social transition may not mean "changing" from one gender to another. Plenty of children do not identify as male *or* female; some are gender-fluid, some are genderqueer, some are bigender, some are agender, and some are simply gender-expansive. For these individuals, the "transition" and "intervention" must be tailored to their particular needs. There may need to be some concrete changes, such as changing names to a more gender-neutral one and/or changing pronouns (possibly to gender-neutral pronouns such as "they" or "ze"). However, other more abstract interventions may be needed for your nonbinary child. These interventions could simply involve having those around them understand how they feel about their gender, and advocating for the use of proper treatment and consideration. This includes being aware of using the gender binary as a "default," and then shifting away from this type of thinking. Language can be an important part of this process. Shifting away from gendered language such as "boys and girls," "ladies and gentlemen," "son/daughter," and "brother/sister," to more gender-neutral terms like "kids," "folks," and "siblings," can make your home a more emotionally safe place for your child. Loved ones should also look at the stated preferences of your child as interventions to make them more comfortable based on how they feel, not "decisions" they are making to be a certain way gender-wise.

Even for the most conscious of parents, learning how to use more gender-neutral language and seeing their child on a limitless spectrum of gender can be an evolutionary process. Be aware of what comes up for you as you adjust to this new way of thinking and communicating. You may realize some concepts about gender have been very deeply engrained in you, and you may find yourself struggling to adjust. Be kind and patient with yourself, acknowledging that mistakes are part of the process. If your child expresses frustration with you or has hurt feelings over your choice of words, stay conscious with them in that moment. Do not let your unconscious mind take over, so that the conflict becomes about you and your own unmet needs. If you stay with your child, you can more easily connect to the feelings your words brought up in them, which facilitates a deeper understanding between you and your child. Your nonbinary child may often feel misunderstood, in society, at school, and so on. They desperately need to feel safe and understood at home. Partner with them in this need and acknowledge when your words do not meet that need. This does not make you a bad parent; it makes you human. What your child needs in that moment is not a perfect parent, but genuine compassion, understanding, and connection.

PARENT PROCESS AND SOCIAL TRANSITION

Social transition can be a positive time for families of transgender children, as it is often a time when parents witness their child blossom, often becoming happier than they were before. At the same time, social transition of a child can be difficult for parents, because it tends to open them up to more feedback from others. Additionally, even if the parents were becoming used to the idea that their child is a different gender than originally thought, concrete shifts such as name and pronoun changes can elicit strong emotional responses. Parents often have to get used to letting go of a name they lovingly selected when their child was born, and change pronouns to those that feel foreign and awkward at first. Remind yourself that every time you use the name and pronouns that are reflective of your child's gender identity, you are giving your child a gift of loving kindness and reinforcing your complete acceptance. Take care of yourself as you do this, acknowledging that all feelings are welcome and normal. Talk to friends and family about your feelings. Talk to other parents who have gone through a similar process. Knowing how they relate to this process can be hugely comforting.

THE TRAIN HAS LEFT THE STATION

Once a child or youth is able to assert who they really are, and comes to understand others may be able to see them this way, there often becomes an urgency surrounding the transition. While parents may feel the idea has just been introduced and all parties need time to adjust/contemplate/plan, it may seem as though the child is off and running. This can be likened to a train leaving the station; parents sometimes feel left on the platform wondering what happened. The child is running full steam ahead, celebrating their true self and making sure everyone else knows about it.

Remind yourself that your child is their own being with their own sovereign thoughts and desires. Ultimately, in regard to their gender, they are their own engineer. Before the train gets too far out of sight, run fast and jump on board.

The conscious parent's task at this moment is to recognize the two impulses (child's and parent's) and how different they are: One wants to speed up and the other wants to slow down. Being aware of this doesn't mean you should actually try to get the child to slow down; it means recognizing the feelings you have in yourself when you feel things are moving too quickly.

This doesn't mean you will feel as excited or urgent as your child. It means you will be staying close to your child to observe, affirm, and assist as needed. You will remain close to witness the journey and experience it with them, even in the moments when you want it to slow down. Watching their face as they drive that train may be the most important moments of education you need during the journey.

FEAR REGARDING TRANSITION

Fear of facilitating or supporting a child's transition often seems to be influenced by external factors. Fear of the reaction of significant others, family members, coworkers, or society at large can all play a part. If the parent's fear of transition remains greater than the desire to allow the child to live authentically, it can prolong the transition process, often to the detriment of the child's mental health. It may even influence the child to give up on the idea of transitioning, or resign themselves to try to be happy in their assigned gender at birth. (Many transgender adults can tell you they have tried this, even temporarily, and it does not typically result in a happy, authentic life.) Having a transgender child decide not to transition is not necessarily cause for relief; it may be a cause for concern. Not transitioning due to fear of reactions or out of desire to please others is the recipe for an unhappy future. Over time, with increased societal understanding of what it means to be transgender and extensive depathologizing of the concept, the relationship between who someone is and how they can live authentically will become much easier.

For some parents, deciding to allow their child to socially transition is easy, even if the process is a challenging one. Once their child's gender identity is realized, transitioning to be recognized as their true gender is a natural next step.

For many transgender children, transitioning is a positive process and one that brings relief, joy, and satisfaction. Parents may have mixed emotions; some difficult feelings might be triggered by their personal attachment to their child's assigned gender at birth—while at the same time they experience great relief/joy about seeing their child happy.

Some parents find themselves in the unique position of seeing that their child would probably benefit from social transition, and may want to transition, but remains too reluctant to assert this. In these cases, the fear of transition may be higher in the child than the parent. This can be quite a tricky place for a parent to be, particularly if they are worried others will accuse them of "pushing" their child to transition. This is yet another tightrope; how to honor your child's process and timeline while minimizing their distress. At this stage, parents may need to focus on enhancing their child's overall self-esteem and self-confidence while providing information about the available options. You might need to remind yourself that even though you can clearly see what needs to happen, you cannot control your child's own process. Just as you are encouraged to embrace and affirm your child's need to transition, you must also embrace and affirm your child's need to wait. Stay connected to your child. If you feel confident that you have given them the tools and the information they need to pursue transition if needed, rest assured your child will assert themselves when it is right for them. Honor their self-determination and their own wisdom about timing. They need to know you are there to walk with them, wherever they may be on the journey.

Medical Transition

Prepubescent transgender youth do not typically undergo medical interventions when transitioning. There are usually no medical interventions at all until the transgender youth enters the first stages of puberty. At this stage, the main focus of medical interventions is preventative: to prevent the transgender youth from going through the puberty associated with their assigned sex, so that their body more accurately represents their gender identity. Transgender individuals who transition after puberty often pursue more medical interventions, partly to "undo" some effects of puberty such as facial hair for transfeminine individuals, and breast development for transmasculine individuals.

PUBERTY SUPPRESSION

Transgender youth are typically aware of what their assigned puberty might entail and are quite relieved when they realize there are interventions to prevent this. Pubertal suppression by way of hormone blockers (also referred to as "hormone suppression therapy") during pre/early puberty block the hormones associated with one's assigned sex and prevent/pause development of gender markers that are incongruent with one's gender identity. Hormone blockers are ideally administered when a transgender youth is entering Tanner Stage 2 (see sidebar) of puberty to prevent any changes from happening.

The Tanner Stages of puberty are guidelines to help doctors and parents determine what stage of puberty a youth is in based on pubic hair development, breast and genital growth, and so on. At Tanner Stage 1, a child is prepubescent. Tanner Stages 2–5 document the many changes that come with puberty until an individual reaches adulthood (post-puberty).

Of course, older transgender youth who have already entered a later stage of puberty can benefit from having the puberty process paused or halted. This can help address the dysphoria that comes with the puberty of their assigned sex, which can be quite distressing. Pubertal suppression is only administered with parental informed consent. Parents often feel relatively comfortable with this intervention because it is reversible; once the hormone suppression therapy is stopped, the youth's assigned puberty will resume. This can serve to satisfy any doubts parents may have about proceeding with hormone therapy, allow time for parents/family to get counseling and support as needed, and explore the full range of treatment options with the youth.

Hormone suppression therapy is not just appropriate for transgender adolescents who are seeking transition. It can also be very helpful for those who are gender-fluid, because this therapy gives the individual time to establish some gender constancy in regard to their physical form.

The most commonly used hormone blocker for these purposes is Lupron (leuprolide acetate), administered via monthly injection. Implants of histrelin, a different GnRH (gonadotropin-releasing hormone) analogue, are also an option that can last a year or more. This therapy is costly and unattainable for many if having to pay out of pocket. Depending on state laws regarding transgender care, or how your physician codes the condition, insurances may or may not cover this treatment. Policies and laws are changing, but you may need to work with your provider, insurance company, and even state policies to get your child's hormone suppression therapy covered.

HORMONE THERAPY

After hormone suppression therapy, if the youth's desire to transition has remained, the next step is hormone replacement therapy. Hormones (estrogen or testosterone) would be administered to initiate puberty that reflects the individual's true gender. This therapy produces some much-desired gender markers to help your adolescent assert themselves as their true gender in society. These gender markers include but are not limited to a deeper voice and facial hair for transgender males, and a more curvaceous figure for transgender females. Without the needed physical help from hormones, dysphoria can be quite escalated. Hormones are ideally administered at the age when most teenagers undergo pubertal changes. This allows your transgender preteen/teen to undergo these changes along with their peers, which is developmentally and socially significant. Being a "late bloomer" can be tough for cisgender teenagers; it can be dangerous for dysphoric teens who are struggling to assert their true gender identity.

Unique Considerations

Not all transgender individuals desire hormone therapy. Depending on one's gender identity and where they land on the spectrum, their desire for gender markers and gender presentation will vary. Just as all gender identities are valid, so are the decisions about options regarding medical transition. You may one day need to help your youth navigate decisions about hormone therapy while they struggle to relate to one specific hormone and the changes it brings.

PEACE FOR PARENTS

Your youth's gender therapist can help you (and your youth) decide if hormone blockers/therapy is the right way to go, and if so, when to start. Making this move can help your youth find relief for other stressors such as anxiety regarding impending puberty, social anxiety regarding how they are "read," and dysphoria. Many times the preadolescent or adolescent may express being ready for hormone blockers or hormones before the parents feel ready. The gender therapist can help parents walk through many of the anxious and difficult feelings that may arise during this significant decision-making time.

Parents are usually (and understandably) attached to their youth's body just the way it is, and they may be resistant to changes that are not in line with what they expected for the course of pubertal changes. This is yet another exercise in conscious parenting: realizing you are not only separate from your youth's spirit, but also their body. While you may have played a part in creating your child, their body is not yours. It is theirs. Taking care of yourself while you acknowledge this separateness and relinquishing control of their body is an essential part of the process.

Visualization

If you can, make a recording of yourself reading the following visualization exercise, and then listen to it when you are alone and comfortable. Close your eyes and let the words paint a picture for you.

> You are treading water, holding your child. There is no urgency yet, but you can feel yourself tiring. Your legs are starting to burn,

and your breath is getting heavier. You hold on to your child a little tighter, but this inhibits your ability to tread effectively. You see two very small sandbars, several feet apart. You feel reluctant to place your child on one and stand on the other, as you would rather share one. You try to climb up on one, still holding on to your child. It is too small for the two of you; it is only meant for one person. Reluctantly, but resolutely, you place your child on one sandbar and swim to the other. Once you are standing on it, you look at your child. They look back at you, smiling. The sun glints off of the water and onto their face and hair. You breathe a sigh of relief; they are okay being separate. They are sovereign, and they are whole. It is those times when they can be separate that you can see them best of all.

DOWN THE ROAD

Depending on the timing of medical interventions for your transgender youth, their medical transition may eventually involve surgery to undo the effects of their assigned puberty. For transgender boys who had some chest development prior to pubertal suppression, or for those who became consciously aware of being transgender after puberty had taken hold, chest dysphoria can be quite pronounced. They may express a strong (and often urgent) desire for "top surgery." This is not simply a mastectomy; it is the construction of a male chest. An experienced and qualified surgeon understands this important distinction. For transgender girls, depending on how much effect their assigned male puberty influenced the development of their facial features and laryngeal prominence, you may hear them express a desire for facial feminization surgery or other medical interventions. It is important to walk with them through these desires, balancing affirmation and access to appropriate medical care with self-acceptance.

Genital surgery, often referred to as "bottom surgery" or "gender affirmation surgery," is something that may be considered when an individual gets older. This is the construction of genitals that are more congruent with one's true gender identity. The timing of the surgery often depends upon the level of dysphoria, health of the individual, and readiness for understanding the risks and benefits of surgery. As with hormone therapy, not all transgender individuals opt to get genital surgery. Some transgender individuals are happy with their bodies just as they are. Others do not feel ready for the invasiveness of the surgery or the recovery process. It is a very personal decision, and one that should be honored based on each individual's unique needs and desires.

Important Points to Consider

There are a wide range of interventions that can be implemented. These interventions are based on the needs of each individual. As hard as it is, as a parent you must do your best to avoid getting overwhelmed with the many options out there. Take one thing at a time, and the next needed step will show itself as you continue down this journey. The most important thing is to utilize interventions that address any distress you see in your transgender youth.

- O Interventions for gender-expansive and transgender youth can range from watching, waiting, and affirming to social and medical transition.

- O Since one does not decide to be transgender, transitioning should not be looked at as a decision but rather an intervention based on one's true gender identity.

- O The interventions you choose to employ for your transgender youth can allow them to live fully and authentically.

- O The child is the expert on their gender identity, and a gender therapist can help you navigate the gender journey.

- O Social and medical transitions are often necessary for children with a binary gender identification. Interventions for children who are nonbinary include understanding their unique gender identity and advocating for their resulting needs.

CHAPTER 10

Outside Influences

Since you are raising your gender-expansive child within an extended family and within a larger society, you will have to navigate outside influences when it comes to your child. At times you will likely feel "accountable" to explain your child and perhaps justify your own way of responding to them or raising them. While having outside support can be invaluable, trying to get certain others to understand your child can at times seem like a formidable task. This chapter will help you understand how to best navigate these challenges while taking care of yourself and prioritizing your child's happiness.

Coping with Difficult Responses

The responses you get from others in regard to your child's gender expansiveness (either not conforming to the expectations typically held for their assigned gender or being transgender) may vary widely. Also, the responses you experience from others may vary depending on many different factors, which include but are not limited to culture, religion, socioeconomic status, and geographical location. In more liberal areas, parents tend to feel that the responses of others are largely supportive and better than expected. These positive responses can be a source of joy and support along the journey.

While the majority of responses you get are hopefully positive, you must be prepared for negative responses, as these can be far more difficult to navigate. The most important thing when it comes to dealing with difficult responses is knowing you can't control the responses of others, and that you can remain separate from the feelings of others. If you find yourself trying to control their response, or if you are trying to force them to see things as you do, take pause. Your unmet needs or your ego may have been triggered, causing your unconscious mind to enter the situation. Even though the responses of others may be difficult to bear at times, allow them the space and respect they need to experience their own authentic response. With your help, they may come around in their own time.

FEAR

If your child is gender-expansive, and their gender expression is outside of what is expected for their assigned gender role, then those who care about your child may experience fear. They may wonder why you are not intervening in such a way that would modify your child's behavior/expression, and therefore reduce the risk of the child being hurt or teased in the future. You may hear concerns that mimic your own past concerns, and this may stir up feelings of doubt in you that, in turn, make you wonder if you are doing the right thing. Stay within yourself. This fear is not yours. It is coming from someone else who is not as far along in the journey as you are.

Fear is often a huge component in the reactions of others in response to the news that a child is transgender. When a parent reveals their child's true gender identity and/or plans to transition, there may be three participants in that conversation: the parent, the loved one, and Fear. Of course, how much fear is present depends upon the nature of the relationship between the child, parent, and loved one, and the worldview of the loved one.

Any type of change can trigger the fear reaction. Many people prefer things to remain just as they are: familiar, stable, and predictable. Change that is unexpected and unwelcome can signal something that is out of one's control. Family members and friends may feel out of control regarding this issue, powerless to change it, and sometimes powerless to understand. Many loved ones eventually realize it is the decision of the parent to help with the transition, despite their resistance. (Ultimately, the goal is to get them to a place that recognizes everything is okay, and that there is nothing to fear or try to change.) Many loved ones fear they are "losing" a child they love very much, and may not recognize the person the child becomes. Many fear the child they care about will regret such a significant transition. Most, at some point, will worry about the safety of the transgender child.

In addition to these specific fears, having a child come out as transgender can threaten one's previously held beliefs about gender. Those who could previously organize gender into two neat little boxes can be thrown by the concept that gender can be fluid and dynamic. It can cause people to question core beliefs about something they always thought they understood. Challenging core beliefs can make people uncomfortable. The less the person understands, the more fear will be present to take the place of knowledge and comprehension. The ideas and worst-case scenarios people create often cause more fear than a simple void of not knowing what is going to happen.

Fear can whisper; fear can shout. Fear may be ever present in the journey your loved ones take to acceptance, or it may only rear its ugly head every now and again. When fear does come, recognize it for what it is. See the fear, which may be disguised as anger and masked in a lashing out you don't deserve. Understand and expect the fear, as fear is/was likely a part of *your* journey, too. Let your loved one know that you're in this together. Eventually you can help fear be on its way.

SHOCK

Some loved ones are shocked when they hear the news of a transgender child's true gender identity and/or plans to transition. They may experience this shock even if they have witnessed the child's gender-expansive behavior for years. Shock itself is an intense emotion, and therefore can cause impulsive, insensitive reactions. Shock can impede the "filter" that people have most of the time. This impulsivity may cause others to say the first things that come to their minds. Saying the first thing that comes to one's mind when high emotions are involved is usually not a good idea. When you are disclosing about your child, you are in a vulnerable place, and things that are said in those first few moments of disclosure may be something you remember for years to come.

This is why disclosing through e-mails or letters can often be easier. As much as face-to-face communication has its value, this may just be one of those situations where a letter is more appropriate. A letter gives you the opportunity to really think about what to say and how to say it. (A letter can also be revised many times, unlike saying it all out loud!) Those on the receiving end get to read and absorb the news before a conversation takes place. Having some time and space to process new information is a great way to avoid saying the first thing that comes to mind. It allows the recipient of the letter to react without you knowing everything about their reaction. There are some things that are simply better left unsaid (and unheard!). See Appendix A for a sample disclosure letter, written on behalf of the parents of a young transgender child.

When preparing to disclose, it's important to prepare yourself for possible hurtful statements from others, particularly if you expect them to be shocked. Preparing is not about anticipating negative responses to the extent of being fearful or even holding back from sharing, rather it is about helping you anticipate what may be in store so that you can take better care of yourself in the moment. (This is more a task for the adult mind than the child mind, as the developmentally advanced adult mind is capable of understanding more complex social situations and emotions.) Remind yourself that strong reactions can be part of the process, and things will almost certainly get better over time. It's important to have answers and boundaries ready to go so that you are not caught off-guard. Additionally, it may be helpful to try to understand the feelings the other person might have, which will help you better understand the motivation behind the statements they may make. This understanding may make their statements easier to tolerate and make you less likely to "take them on" as your own. Remember, you are identifying the feelings of someone else, not yours.

The Cold Lake Analogy

Picture this: you want to go swimming in a very cold lake. You first stick your toe in, shiver a bit, but forge ahead. Slowly, inch by inch, you submerge your body in the lake. It's uncomfortable, but you're determined to take a swim. Once you have been treading water for about five to ten minutes, the water seems to feel much warmer. Eventually, it's hard to remember you thought the water was cold at all. You see your friend and yell, "Come on in, the water's fine!" They stick their toe in. Their response? "Are you serious? It's freezing!" Looking at you submerged in the water, smiling, your friend just can't understand what it is you are doing, or how it feels good to you. This can be the way a loved one looks upon the transition; by the time the parent discloses about their transgender child, the shock has long passed. They have been adjusting to the "water" for much longer.

One thing to keep in mind from this analogy is that the water both people are feeling is the exact same water; it's the same temperature. The difference in the interpretations of how the water feels largely comes from how long each has been getting used to it. Give your loved one some time to adjust. Before you know it, they may be comfortably treading water right there beside you.

Opinions Galore

No matter where your child lands along the gender expression or gender identity spectrums, their expression or assertions may elicit others to share their opinions on the matter. Suddenly, everyone is an expert! You may hear phrases that start with the dreaded, "Why don't you just . . ." or "If it were me, I would just . . . ." As a conscious parent raising a gender-expansive child, the only "just" you are working on is the "just" letting your child *be*. The other "justs" aren't as simple, and certainly may not be in line with a gender-affirmative approach. "Justs" don't tend to work with any child, because every child is different.

You may hear feedback about how you are "allowing" your child to be gender-expansive, which may have the implication this is a bad thing. Others may insinuate you are simply not setting appropriate parenting boundaries, and that you are letting your child walk all over you by picking their gender expression and asserting their gender identity. It may be hard to avoid getting defensive in these moments. It is in these moments that it is most important for you to stay grounded and remain connected to your truth within.

Are you "allowing" your child to express and assert themselves in a way they feel is in line with their authentic self? Yes. Of course you are. Gender expression and identity is not something that should be controlled, lest you want your child to modify who and how they are to please others as a general practice.

In addition to suggestions that you have allowed your child's gender expansiveness through permissive parenting, you may get the antagonistic implication that you have created or encouraged it. If you had all assigned male children, and should one be gender-expansive or transgender, people may say that perhaps you created this with your desire for a daughter. Or they may say that since you weren't opposed to your child being gender-expansive, your response not only didn't discourage it but encouraged and maintained it. Loved ones may cite examples when they witnessed you suggest something that was in line with your child's gender preferences. They may remind you of an item you bought your child that suited their gender expression and not their assigned gender at birth. Look closely at these behaviors. Do you see what they see? Do you see cause for concern that you encouraged something that should have instead been extinguished or modified? Or do you see that you were you acting as a loving, conscious parent: affirming and thoughtfully supporting your child's passions? If you stay within yourself and remain true to your understanding of yourself, your child, and a gender-affirming stance, then you can most certainly rest assured in the knowledge you were simply doing the latter.

When the unconscious mind takes over, you may be bowled over by raw emotion. You may feel extremely hurt and defensive. You may have a hard time separating the negative feedback from yourself. While it is natural to feel hurt at times when you don't feel supported, overwhelming emotion that pulls you from the present often carries with it some sort of unmet need. What is your unmet need in that moment? To be reinforced that you are in fact being a good parent? To be affirmed or nurtured yourself? Tune into yourself and see if you can find a way to acknowledge that need while remaining separate from the feedback.

If you are feeling defensive, chances are your ego is involved. Letting your ego take the wheel results in less conscious thinking and a lower state of overall functioning. Your ego can separate you from everyone and everything else. The more aware you are of your ego, the easier it is to become more conscious.

When you are processing outside opinions, you are essentially experiencing a parallel process to what you want your child to be able to do when it comes to the feedback of others throughout their lifetime. You want your child to be able to stay true to themselves even in the midst of opposition or questioning. Therefore, it is essential for you to do the same.

When your sense of self-worth is based on and connected to your authentic inner voice, the more liberated you are from the impact of external influences. The orientation from which you operate should be from your inner self so that you are not controlled by what others say in regard to your child's gender identity. Communicate this orientation to your child and model it for them.

MICROAGGRESSIONS

According to the recent "Diversity in the Classroom" study performed at UCLA, microaggressions are "the everyday verbal, nonverbal, and environmental slights, snubs, or insults, whether intentional or unintentional, that communicate hostile, derogatory, or negative messages to target persons based solely upon their marginalized group membership." Microaggressions are not often overtly hostile, so they can be difficult to recognize. If you feel confronted, feel as though you have to explain certain facets of your existence (or your child's), or come away from a conversation feeling uneasy or unnerved, then chances are you may have experienced a microaggression. You and your child exist separately from others and their opinions. Your child does not exist to educate others, especially to the detriment of yourself or your child. You do not owe others explanations, especially with the purpose of making them more comfortable. The more you can recognize microaggressions, the better able you will be to separate yourself from them and lay the responsibility back into the hands of the offending person. This will be a valuable skill to teach your child as they get older, particularly if their gender presentation does not conform to mainstream societal standards.

The Truth

Some of the difficulty that may arise when contending with outside influences in response to having a transgender child may be the difference in opinion of what constitutes the "truth" about gender. What defines someone's true gender? Historically, it was thought that one's true gender is defined by genitalia at birth. We now know that a person's true gender is the one that exists within, the psychological sense of self. This may be something you need to explore with your child, and be sure you understand yourself, before you can feel equipped to respond to assertions about the "truth," much less help your child to do the same.

THE EVOLUTION OF UNDERSTANDING

For children, where does "truth" come from? Initially, the truth tends to come from the adults who are in charge of them. Children will often accept the truth as told by parents, and it can be quite confusing and anxiety-provoking to experience an internal "truth" that one's parents are refuting. Children want to have a shared reality with their parents; it often feels safer that way.

How many children are told their reality of gender from a very young age? How many children are told, "You can't wear a dress, *you're a boy!*" or "Of course you don't have a penis, *you're a girl!*" These parents may believe they are teaching their children the "truth," when in fact they may be doing just the opposite.

Often, those "you're a boy" and "you're a girl" statements are absorbed by the young children as truth. Additionally, they communicate to children that there are only two possibilities for gender: boy or girl. Children absorb this as truth, too, and it leaves out many true identities that fall outside of the gender binary.

For children, it will often seem to them that anything other than what their trusted guardians are telling them must be untrue, therefore causing them to question their own internal feelings. Additionally, they may feel that something they are experiencing that differs from what their parents are telling them must be something to keep to themselves. Only a minority of gender-expansive and transgender children are insistent and assert their truth over the contrary statements of their parents. In looking back to the early days of your child's gender journey, were there some things you communicated to your child as "truth" that you may need to now rectify?

It's okay to go back and explain your own evolution of the understanding of what constitutes one's true gender. Focus on what you now understand to be true, and what needs to be done in order for your child to live their authentic truth.

"HONESTY" AS IT RELATES TO GENDER

Young children are concrete thinkers, and are not capable of abstract thinking until they get older. While bodies are concrete, the gender identity in one's mind is more of an abstract concept, making it less tangible. In addition to this, as a part of a child's moral development, the importance of telling the truth is given much significance. Lying or deceiving someone is frowned upon, and children are often punished for it.

As a child gets older, they develop the understanding of truth, honesty, and conscience. This moral development and ability to grasp abstract concepts can influence a child's ability to understand their own gender identity, assert their true gender and desire to transition, and/or communicate their need to be read in larger society as their true gender.

An enlightened, insightful transgender adult may begin the process of transitioning and will likely enjoy being recognized as the gender identity that matches their internal experience of gender. For example, if a transmasculine transgender individual starts the transition process and is addressed in the grocery store as "sir," he may feel pleased. Does he feel deceitful, as though he is not telling the truth? Not likely. For him, he understands his true gender identity is male, thereby making it okay to be seen as male and assert himself as male.

This is a bit trickier for a child, particularly a latency-age child who is learning the concepts of right and wrong, honesty, and the concept of guilt. Some parents notice their child (if they have not transitioned) get angry when they are read as being the gender that is more in line with their gender expression (and possibly identity). They are surprised, thinking this would have made their child happy. If the child gets mad, parents often look to this as a possible clue that their child is not transgender. Instead, this reaction may have to do more with concrete thinking and the desire to be "honest." (On the other hand, there are kids who are thrilled when they are perceived as their authentic gender and would never tell the stranger otherwise! Everyone is different.)

The point of reference a child has in regard to what is honest depends upon what they have been told about gender, what makes someone a boy, a girl, or if they have been given options that include feeling both or neither. One way to help children understand that it's okay to be true to themselves is to explain the difference between anatomical sex (body) and authentic gender identity (heart and brain), as well as the fact that their authentic gender identity is who they "truly" are. This gives them the green light to relax and know that when they assert their authentic gender, they are in fact telling the truth.

Some transgender kids are told by peers (after transition), "But you're *really* a girl" or "You're *really* a boy." These peers aren't necessarily being mean; they are simply asserting what they know concretely (body) and are enforcing what they think is the truth. This is why it is so important to help transgender children understand that who they really are is who they are in their "brain" and their "heart," and then also give them language to help their peers understand.

When talking about bodies, it may be helpful to reference your child's (or any transgender person's) body in terms of when they were a baby. This may feel somewhat less invasive than talking about their body as it is now that they are older. "When you were born, your body made the doctor think you were a _____." Or, when explaining to other children, "When they were born, they had the body of a _____. Now we understand they have the heart and brain of a _____."

In general, the focus has to be on a societal shift of understanding what someone's gender really is. If gender continues to be mistaken as being synonymous with sex, then confusion, misunderstandings, and stigma will continue.

Disclosure

If you are not personally part of the LGBT (lesbian, gay, bisexual, and transgender) community, then you may not have experience with disclosing personal information about being a part of a minority group to others. "Coming out" is a term usually used to describe revealing a personal aspect of oneself, usually in reference to sexual orientation or gender identity. If you are the parent of a transgender child, you will likely at some point find yourself in the position to disclose either your child's intention to transition (whatever that may look like) or their history of transition.

When you disclose, or get ready to disclose, be consciously aware of the thoughts and feelings this brings up in you. Remind yourself that you are not asking for approval from others; you are simply informing them of something significant going on in your (and your child's) life. When you can consciously take ownership of your decisions, you activate certain parts of your brain that help promote inner peace. It is important to take full conscious responsibility for your decisions so that you are not triggered into a less conscious state of mind by the reactions of others.

If you are disclosing to someone you care very much about, it is a good idea to provide information from the start or steer them in the right direction of where to find information. There are a lot of resources available and you do not need to be the one to provide all the information, let alone answer all the questions. However, taking the time to explain your journey to understanding and accepting your child's true gender identity, and all the feelings (both positive and negative) that went with it, may be just the information the other person needs to "get it." This is another reason why disclosing in a letter can help you provide important, personal information without burning yourself out by having to do it over and over again.

There are a lot of factors that impact how others receive the news that a young loved one is transgender. One of the biggest obstacles is a lack of knowledge. When there is a void of knowledge, a plethora of opinions, guesses, and myths can take its place, all of which can contribute to a negative response or a difficult processing of the news.

SOME GET IT, SOME DON'T

Even when resources are provided and personal feelings shared, many still do not "get it." Some simply cannot wrap their brains around the concept. Some are too deeply rooted in their own experiences, some are very attached to the concept of the gender dichotomy, and some can only see what is concrete. There's a difference between having information and "getting it." "Getting it" takes some ability to see gray areas, and understand that gender is not black and white. There are also a variety of other things that can contribute to one's ability to "get it." These include personal experience, background, basic ability to appreciate those who are different, religion, empathy, and the ability to see life from another's point of view.

In those cases where your loved one doesn't seem to understand even after you've done a lot of explaining and given many resources, tell them that you love them and ask what you would like from them in regard to you and your child in order to maintain a relationship. If they love you, operating from a stance of love and compassion can go a long way even if they don't "get it."

How much energy should be put into trying to make others "get it"? After making a reasonable effort to explain yourself and your child, and perhaps providing the basic information about being transgender, it is perfectly reasonable for you to set a boundary. Too much explaining and educating can be depleting for you as the parent, as you likely have multiple other demands that require your energy. It's also important to allow others the space to come around on their own. (You have probably been down a similar journey yourself with *your* initial reactions of resistance/doubt/ fear, and then eventual acceptance.) Acknowledge the possibility that the other person may not come around.

"OUT" VERSUS UNDISCLOSED

Some transgender children and adults choose to be openly transgender and are "out" to most everyone. This includes celebrities who have transitioned, advocates in the transgender community, and people who are simply vocal about this aspect of their identity. In this sense, their transgender experience is disclosed. Others remain quiet about it to those who do not know their history, and disclose only under certain circumstances. Their transgender experience can be described as "undisclosed."

Parents and children may differ about how disclosed or undisclosed they want the child's transgender experience to be. This is yet another offshoot of the path you must navigate. You may feel strongly about sharing your child's transgender experience in order to advocate for the community and educate others, but your child may be intensely private about it and may not want you to share it. In the end, what your child desires is what must be honored and respected, as it is your child's personal preference regarding the information that matters most. Conversely, your child may be very open about their history and you may feel more of a need to be private about it. In this case, the focus needs to be on exploring the risks and benefits of disclosure, assessing any safety concerns that may be present, and determining the ability of your child to make an informed consent decision about disclosing. Ultimately, allowing your child to be open about their transgender experience may be best for their mental health.

If you have a transgender child who is either very private about their experience or is contemplating who to tell, partner with your child so they know you will help support them in their decision-making process. As always, keep yourself focused on the fact that your child is a sovereign being who will have desires about privacy or disclosure that may differ from yours. As children get older, some who were very private about being transgender shift to wanting to be more open with their close friends, and some shift all the way to wanting to be advocates for the community. Likewise, young children who were previously very open about being transgender may get more private about it over time. Do not get too attached to how your child feels regarding being disclosed or undisclosed. As with everything, this evolves. In reality, most things are in a constant state of change. Envision yourself as flexible and flowing, like a river, following your child's path.

Private versus Secret

For the child (or parent) who opts to not disclose, it can be helpful to think about the information in terms of private or secret. This distinction can be made in regard to how your child views being transgender, how they decide when/if to share it with others, as well as how to guide your own process of deciding when and if to disclose. Some people are more private in general than others. Some people will tell others most everything about their lives, while others tend to keep most things private. Both are okay, as long as the individual is the one doing the deciding about what to keep private and what to share. Just as most things land on a spectrum, so does one's feelings about exactly how private being transgender is. Some are "out and proud," happy to put a face to this variation of the human condition. Others, on the other end of the spectrum, guard it like a deep, dark secret; one they feel could devastate them if others were to find out. Many people are in the middle of these two extremes, and while they may not share their transgender experience with everyone, they are relatively open about it and comfortable with it.

People on the "secret" end of the spectrum seem to experience more intense dysphoria and internal distress than those who have a more open and accepting relationship with being transgender. If you notice your child being overly secretive about being transgender, for reasons other than realistic safety considerations, it may be in their best interest if you help them shift from "secret" to "private." Also, tune in with yourself to see where you are falling on this spectrum and your reasons for being there.

The best way to explore this with your child is to go over the difference between private and secret, in light of the feelings that may come along with both in regard to their transgender experience. In child terms, *secret* can be defined as something you don't want anyone to know. Explore with your child about how some secrets can be fun, like what you are going to give someone for a present or throwing someone a surprise party. Secrets like these are fun because they are about doing something nice for someone else. Other secrets are not healthy, such as an adult asking a child to keep a secret from their parent. Still other secrets are not good or bad, but might be important to others. For example, if your child's friend tells them who they have a crush on, they might ask your child to keep it a secret.

In child terms, *private* can be considered as something about you that not everyone needs to know or should know. Private information is that which you don't mind sharing with the people you know well and trust, but is not something you would want posted online for everyone to read. Of course, what you look like under your clothes is private. Only a child's parents, guardians, or doctors should see their body for the purpose of keeping them healthy and well taken care of. For older individuals, they can choose with whom to share their bodies in a more intimate setting.

Your child's decision about whether they feel "private" or "secret" about being transgender has to do with how they guard the information in their head and heart. If they feel like it is something about them that they would rather not have everyone know, or would choose only a few people to know, that's okay. If they feel being transgender is a very deep secret that they feel would devastate them if anyone found out, that can negatively affect their mental health. A person who guards being transgender like a deep, dark secret can experience more stress, less self-acceptance, more anxiety, and less confidence. It will be important to talk with your child about why they feel this way about being transgender. Do they consider it a bad thing? If yes, help them begin to have a more positive relationship with themselves and their history. Try to figure out why this feels so secretive to them and how you may be able to help them evolve into considering it private information instead. Feeling like it is private instead of secret may help them feel better about it in general and less worried about others finding out.

Here's a visual for you to share with your child: Think of private information as being kept behind a fence with a gate. There is a boundary around the information, and not everyone can get in. Your child gets to decide for whom to open the gate, or who gets to know their information. Remember that everyone to whom they tell their private information now has a key to the gate, and can let others in without their permission. This is why your child will want to stop and think before they share private information.

As for secret information, help them visualize a castle with a tall wall, drawbridge, and moat with alligators around it. In this castle, they are guarding their secret very aggressively, making sure no one finds out. The problem is, having such walls around you and guarding your secret like that can eventually make you feel very alone. This is why having a fence with a gate (private information) is better than having a guarded castle (secrets).

In addition to empowering your child to have a healthy relationship with being transgender, and thinking wisely but not anxiously about who should know, promote resiliency in regard to how to handle others finding out whom they had not planned to tell. Part of this involves positive thoughts: "I can handle others knowing," "It's just a part of who I am," and "I am awesome just the way I am."

Teach them to stop and think every time someone asks them a question about their private information. They should base their decision upon how they will feel about that person knowing the information, and how they would feel if the information did not stay just with that person. If they decide yes, then they can share the information and ask the other person to keep it private. Remind them that they have no control over whether or not that person will actually keep it private. If they do not feel comfortable sharing, or don't want to risk others sharing this information, they can say something like:

○ "That's personal."

○ "I'd rather not say."

○ "That's private."

RESPONDING TO INAPPROPRIATE QUESTIONS

Given larger society's misconception that gender is synonymous with sex, other people may immediately focus on the sex of your child when you are trying to share about their gender. This not only reveals a misconception that person has about the connection of body and gender identity, but it can feel extremely invasive. After all, talking about the sex of your child involves talking about their private parts! Those who don't know much about gender, gender transition, and so on tend to focus on the concrete, and somewhat more sensationalized, aspects of being transgender, including genital surgery.

Here are a few tips to help you deal with uncomfortable or inappropriate questions:

○ Have a response ready, or an arsenal of responses ready. Be a broken record if you need to be. "I'm not comfortable answering that," "That's a little too personal," "I don't feel comfortable telling you about my child specifically, but I can tell you that some transgender people choose to/choose not to . . . ," or simply "That's private."

○ If the question brings up feelings of frustration or exasperation, take a deep breath. Give yourself space for a response. Remind yourself that the person asking the questions probably does not mean to be offensive.

○ Redirect the person to a more appropriate means of getting their curiosity satisfied. "I appreciate your interest. Let me suggest some websites/books/blogs, etc."

○ A great way to redirect a question is to briefly clarify the difference between gender (mind) and sex (body). You could say, "Actually, that question is more about my child's sex, and I'm trying to tell you about their gender."

If religion is important to you, or an important part of your culture, family life, and so on, it will be important to avoid connecting religion with any negative reactions to your child's gender expansiveness. This may be something you have consciously tried to do, even if historically the religion you are a part of has not been as supportive of human diversity.

As a conscious parent you have likely taken great effort to not have any of your feelings about this be placed on your child. As you share your child's gender expansiveness with others, set firm boundaries in regard to how they connect religion with it as well. If your child begins to associate your religion with judgment or prejudice, they may turn away from something important to you. Additionally, this association has the potential to create an obstacle for your child being able to connect with their own spirituality.

Important Points to Consider

Dealing with outside influences can be one of the trickiest parts of walking down this path with your gender-expansive child. Once you feel like you fully understand what your child is experiencing and needs, having to explain it to others can be challenging. Here are a few thoughts to keep in mind:

○ Difficult reactions can be fueled by fear, shock, or a lack of understanding. It is essential you remain consciously separate from these responses; you do not need to take them on.

○ Being in the know about gender can be a rewarding at times and isolating at others. It can be difficult to have to wait for other people to catch up to your level of understanding, or the level of understanding needed to truly support your child.

○ Disclosure is something that typically goes well, but can be stressful nonetheless.

○ Affirming and supporting your child's preferences is the right thing to do, and helps to create a strong self-confidence in your child. You cannot mold or create a gender identity; this is something that exists on its own.

○ Having you and your child consider their transgender experience as private rather than secret can help you both have a positive relationship with it, and can help you avoid feeling like you have something to guard much of the time.

 **CHAPTER 11**

Siblings and Extended Family

Unless your gender-expansive or transgender child is an only child, there are likely other siblings in your home who also require your love and attention. Paying attention to the needs of all your children, and how they impact each other, can certainly feel like a juggling act. Be forgiving of them, and yourself, during those moments when it feels like a daunting task to give everyone everything they need. In addition, you probably have extended family members who are involved in the welfare of your child, and who care for you as well. Because they care for all of you, choices you make for your gender-expansive child may feel like community property.

Take Them for Ice Cream

At a Gender Spectrum conference there was a workshop on the topic of sibling adjustment. Parents discussed the best way to care for their other children while their transgender child was going through transition. The consensus? "Take them for ice cream!" Taking a sibling for a sweet treat and giving them some one-on-one attention to discuss recent changes in the family may be just the panacea for a child who is feeling unsure, left out, or who has emotions they shouldn't have to cope with alone. When you are out, one-on-one if possible, talk with them about their gender-expansive sibling. If the sibling is expansive in gender expression but is not undergoing gender transition, this conversation would be a good time to explore the gender "rules" that society tends to try to impose on kids, and why they are too restricting. Reiterate that "toys/colors/clothing are for all kids" so they can rest assured that their sibling is not actually breaking any rules. Explore how they can advocate for their sibling or answer the questions of curious peers.

If their sibling is socially transitioning, talk with your child about this. Explore how they feel to have a brother now instead of a sister, a sister instead of a brother, or a sibling who no longer identifies with their assigned gender at birth. Ask if this feels like a loss to them and normalize this feeling if it does. Ask what the hardest part has been. Ask what the best part has been. Ask about worries, questions, and concerns. Depending on the age of the sibling, concerns may be minimal or concerns may be plenty. The younger they are, the more flexible their thinking will be, and the more quickly they may adjust to the changes. The older they are, the more concerned they may be about how this will impact them and their social standing.

Most importantly, talk with them about *them*. Ask what has been their favorite part about school, ask what they've done recently that they are proud of, ask which peers they are spending most of their time with. Make this a sacred time when it's all about *them*, especially if those moments have been coming all too infrequently. Take the time to just sit, savoring the sweetness of the ice cream, the beauty of the surroundings, and the precious time together. Allow space for your other child to just be with you and have your undivided attention.

If ice cream isn't your thing, there are plenty of other ways to spend quality time with your gender-expansive child's sibling. Take them to some sort of ceramic or art shop where the goal is to create something while you talk. Go for a walk on the beach or on a hike, where the focus is on both the conversation and the surroundings. Children and adolescents tend to open up more when they can be doing something while they talk.

Honoring a Sibling's Process

Just as everything is on a spectrum, so are the reactions to a sibling's transition. Usually, young siblings adjust relatively quickly. Internalized inhibitions and fears of societal stigma are low at this age, and the child typically responds well, out of love for their sibling. Additionally, because a child's thought process can be relatively pure and uncomplicated, the concept of adjusting to the new gender of their sibling can be surprisingly simple. You may find that your young child is your transgender child's biggest advocate, and even regulates *your* accurate use of pronouns.

If the child is older, the adjustment process will likely be somewhat fettered by worries about what other people might think. Siblings are often very tied to the concept of having a brother or sister, and resist accepting that this is different than what they thought or knew to be true. Even if your transgender child was never interested in things typically associated with that of their assigned gender at birth, their siblings may have held out hope that one day they would be interested in doing those things with them.

No matter what the sibling's process is, honor it. If they are ready to move forward quicker than you expected (or quicker than you are!), embrace it. If they fight against it, express grief and loss, honor it. These are real emotions and are not to be negotiated away. Rest assured that the acute resistance and pain they feel is temporary, as was yours if you experienced (or are experiencing) the same.

The one thing you must insist upon to your transgender child's sibling is that transphobic or deliberately hurtful comments about their gender will simply not be tolerated. Your child should feel free to express emotion, especially to parents. But hurtful comments can damage your transgender child's self-image and the sibling relationship beyond repair.

Remember that your other children will absorb your energy about their transgender sibling, your transgender child. If you want them to be accepting, you must model acceptance and have it be genuine. They will watch and learn from you about how to view having a transgender family member, and they will watch how you handle it with others. Model a strong, confident, positive attitude so that they may absorb this attitude as well.

WORKSHEETS

Worksheets can help children understand the concept of being transgender and the transition process. Worksheets simplify concepts and explain them in easy-to-understand language, and they facilitate conversations between the child and adults. Fill-in-the-blank worksheets provide a great way to find out what is on a child's mind. (A worksheet for a child adjusting to a loved one's transition can be found in Appendix D.)

A simple way of explaining being transgender to a child can sound something like this:

> "Some people are born with boy bodies and have the hearts and brains of girls. Some people are born with girl bodies and have the hearts and brains of boys." (Depending on the child, you may need to explain that some children feel like both a boy and a girl while some feel like neither.) "When this happens, the person can feel sad. It makes them happier to change the way people see them to match

how they feel inside their hearts and brains. They may want others to use a different name for them and different words to describe them, like 'he' instead of 'she', 'she' instead of 'he', or something else altogether. When people they love use the names and the words they want, they feel happy."

After explaining what it means to be transgender and transition, go over the included worksheet and have them "fill in the blanks." You may write the answers for them if they are too young to write. These worksheets are not only good for helping siblings but they can help cousins, friends, and neighbors of the transgender child.

Children often have a much easier time understanding gender and gender transition than adults do. This may be due to the malleable, adaptable nature of a child's brain. When adults fear they will confuse or upset the child by explaining gender transition to them, this is usually a product of projection. Adults, even with their abilities for abstract thought, typically struggle more with understanding the transition and remembering to use pronouns than a child does.

Some may argue that very young children should not be privy to information about transgender individuals, gender transition, and so on, and that perhaps they are too young to understand. It is important to remember that gender is not pathological, and there is nothing wrong with being transgender. Some may worry the concept is too advanced or too mature, possibly connecting it with sexuality. Remember, sexuality and gender identity are two totally separate things. There is nothing inherently sexual about gender identity. Normalizing being transgender is essential to the health and well-being of your transgender child, and positively influences the climate of society in regard to gender transition.

Handling Expressions of Concern

Beyond siblings, your family is almost assuredly made up of extended family members who are invested in your immediate family. Depending on the culture, history, and types of relationships in your extended family, the nature and frequency of input given by extended family members will vary. Most extended family members will offer some input when it comes to your gender-expansive child. Some family members may give advice on how to discourage or extinguish gender-expansive behaviors. Some family members may minimize variations in gender identity, citing examples of gender-expansive children who "grew out of it." They may even mention times when they themselves "wanted" to be the other gender.

Many family members will base concerns on what they feel is "common sense." That is, it makes "sense" to them that you can mold a child's behavior regarding gender expression, much like you can mold their behavior in regard to manners, potty training, and so on. It makes "sense" to them that a young child is too young to make a decision about significant elements in their life, much less gender transition. However, they are missing key elements, namely the day-to-day interactions with your child and subtleties of your child's expression of gender that have educated you so well.

> Use your mindfulness techniques to sift through the expressions of concern from extended family members without allowing them to "stick." Notice these concerns, as you would a thought, without accepting them as truth.

You may feel like you need to push back or fight the feedback you are getting from family members, particularly if that feedback is hurting you or if you are feeling protective of your child. Try instead to envision yourself pulling these family members toward you; to your way of thinking, to the knowledge you have because you have absorbed the truth of your child. You can tell them, "I used to think that, too," or "Many people share your concerns." This validates your family member and makes them understand that you think their concerns are rational, even if you don't share them.

VISUALIZATION

If you can, make a recording of yourself reading the following visualization exercise and then listen to it when you are alone and comfortable. Close your eyes and let the words paint a picture for you.

> Imagine yourself in a cold, dark, and dank basement. You shiver and look longingly at the stairs that will lead you out of this dismal place. However, first you stay and take in the many stimuli: the smell, the temperature, the sights. You see things that worry you, smaller things like cobwebs and bigger things like cracks in the wall that look to threaten the stability of the house. Eventually, you slowly climb the staircase and leave the basement. You stand at the top of a staircase, looking out of a window. You can't see all the way to the horizon, but the view is fantastic. The sunlight warms your face, glinting through the window pane. You then have an important conversation with a loved one, and you want them to stay with you at the top of the staircase, looking out the window. Instead, they insist on going into the basement. "Come down here with me," they say; "You need to see all these things, they worry me."
>
> "I've seen them," you say. "I understand. I'm going to stay here in the light."

Setting Boundaries with Love

Part of being a conscious parent is learning how to lovingly accept the care and concern of loved ones while not letting their input derail, drain, or discourage you. You need to be able to validate their concerns without having those concerns distract you from the path you are walking with your child. You can listen to others' points of view while maintaining that anyone who interacts with your child needs to respect their authentic self. In the spirit of staying within yourself, you will need to focus on setting boundaries as an act of self-care, an act of love for yourself and your child. Setting boundaries can be done with love, regardless of the response. The trick is to learn how to tolerate the reactions of those who are kept out by your boundary. Notice the responses, and understand them if possible; you do not need to absorb them or do something to try to "fix" the situation.

Setting boundaries may look and sound like:

- "I hear you, but I need to act on what I think is best for my child."
- "I think we need to agree to disagree on this topic for now."
- "I prefer to continue this conversation at a later time when emotions are not so high."

Children of different genders may be regarded differently in certain cultures, impacting the beliefs about gender expression and identities. Pay attention to how your family's culture is impacting this as well as your feelings about setting boundaries with your loved ones.

A family's culture will most certainly come into play when navigating the responses of others and setting boundaries, particularly when it comes to the role of and respect for older family members. In different cultures, deference to the grandparents or elder family members may be expected. Asserting your own beliefs about how to raise your gender-expansive child may be frowned upon as a sign of disrespect to elders who disagree with the affirmative approach. Practice clear communication with family members as much as possible to minimize the discord surrounding your advocacy for your child.

Pronouns

Pronouns are usually very important in the early stages of social transition. Sometimes pronouns can signify to your child how others are "reading" them. Pronouns also communicate how others are conceptualizing them and their gender. Using the pronoun that accurately reflects their authentic gender is a very concrete way of affirming your child and showing them you honor their authentic self. In the beginning of your child's social transition, you will likely struggle with making the mental adjustment to use the pronouns that best reflect your child's true gender identity. Once you get more used to using these new pronouns, keep in mind that others may just be learning about or coming to understand your child's transition.

BE A SUPERHERO

Those who are willing to assertively and regularly remind others to use the correct pronouns are a special kind of superhero: They are Pronoun Correctors! Pronoun Correctors play a huge role in your child's transition. They model and prompt the correct use of pronouns. Pronoun Correctors show how important it is to use the correct pronouns, and they do not let the "wrong" pronouns slip by unnoticed as if they are unimportant. Typically, a Pronoun Corrector will have far less anxiety than the transitioning child about correcting someone. If you are the parent of a newly transitioning child, you are in the perfect position to be their superhero!

Here are some tips for correcting others' usage of pronouns in regard to your child:

- **Smile when you correct.** Being friendly goes a long way. People will tend to follow your lead more when they don't sense hostility from you or feel that they need to be on the defensive.

- **Correct quietly, but assertively.** State the correct pronoun as simply as possible, ("she"/"he"/"they") and nod as if to indicate, "It's okay, keep going, just wanted to be sure you understand the correct pronoun."

O **Be thoughtful of your target audience and recipient of the correction.** Remember that the objective of correcting pronouns is to help someone understand the gender identity of your child. Model the correct use of pronouns for a group of people who may not be sure about the new pronouns (and who then may appreciate the clarification).

PRONOUNS AND LOVED ONES

Be gentle with your loved ones. Is it necessary to correct every slip? No. If a loved one is trying, and is making a conscious effort to use the correct pronouns, let some slips pass by. After a slip, you can subtly use a correct pronoun later when you are talking, just as a gentle reminder. If slips continue well into the transition, you may need to sit down with the loved one to discuss the importance of pronouns, dysphoria, the concept of "outing" your child. You may also need to make sure they are internally thinking of your child as their true gender, rather than simply trying to use a different pronoun.

If a loved one is not ready to use the new pronouns or has expressed a strong resistance to using them, don't push it. Give them space and time. Use the correct pronouns yourself, and don't comment on their choice of pronouns. Pushing someone before they are ready may close them off to future acceptance and understanding. Watch for signs of distress if inaccurate pronouns are being used in front of your child. If you sense distress, your child may need some space from this person or you may need to be more assertive with the individual.

It may be difficult for your child to understand why someone whom they perceive to love them very much is struggling to use the correct pronouns for them. Ask your child why they think the loved one is making mistakes, and ask about how it makes them feel. Keep in mind the most important part of this conversation is finding out how your child is impacted by the incorrect pronoun usage; this conversation is not really about helping your child understand why the loved one might be struggling to remember. Validate feelings that arise in your child and help them cope with these feelings. Offer comfort and support.

Important Points to Consider

You and your child are likely surrounded by loved ones on this gender journey. There are often siblings and extended family members involved, all of whom are affected by or have opinions about your child's gender expansiveness or transition. When you are interacting with these loved ones, keep the following thoughts in mind:

O Given the attention and energy your gender-expansive child may take, it is important that you also give your child's siblings their own individualized attention and energy. Allow them to have whatever feelings they may have about their gender-expansive sibling, and model acceptance.

O Extended family members may be a support to you during this time, and they also can be an added source of stress. Stay grounded enough to remember you are separate from their responses, and set loving boundaries when necessary for the sake of your own mental health or the health and well-being of your child.

O Pronouns are a very big element to transition, and may be something that extended family members struggle with. Facilitate understanding by making sure family members understand how important it is to use the new pronouns, while caring for your child through the adjustment period.

CHAPTER 12

Helping Your Gender-Expansive Child with Teasing

Most children get teased at one point or another during childhood. Teasing typically happens in a school environment, but can also happen in neighborhoods, other social settings, and online. Sadly, teasing is part of the social culture of children and often occurs away from adult supervision. A gender-expansive child is even more susceptible to teasing given that they tend to behave, dress, or act in a way that can be unexpected or deemed different by other children. Those who are different or in the minority are more likely to be teased than other children. An essential buffering component for a gender-expansive child is to know without a doubt that they are okay exactly as they are, and that those children who are doing the teasing are in the wrong. Building a strong base of confidence at home and fostering an open environment where you can discuss any teasing that occurs, early on, can be very protective for a gender-expansive child.

Teasing versus Bullying

Distinguishing between teasing and bullying is primarily helpful in order for parents to know when and how to intervene. However, the most important thing to do when your child reports being teased or bullied is to connect with their emotional experience of the events and respond to it in a compassionate, thoughtful way. This allows your child to have their own authentic response and emotions associated with what has happened as well as a mindful guide for support (you!).

TEASING

Teasing can come from your child's friends or from peers your child does not consider friends. Teasing can be done in a friendly, fun way that is not meant to be hurtful (even if it is, unintentionally). Teasing can be done in a malicious way, with the purpose being to upset or hurt the recipient. Teasing is typically mild by nature, in both topic and in frequency. Teasing can be infrequent or occasional. Most important, teasing may cause fleeting distress or upset but does not typically cause major distress or trigger an intense need to avoid the teaser.

If your child reports being teased, process the incident with them. Discuss your child's emotional response and any emotional or behavioral tools your child can use to cope with future instances of teasing.

BULLYING

Bullying, unlike teasing, is typically done by someone who is not (or is no longer) your child's friend. Bullying is usually mean-spirited, and its purpose is to upset or cause distress for the child being bullied. Bullying is usually of greater intensity than teasing, in that it often focuses on more sensitive topics and is meant to be personal. Bullying is usually done on a more frequent basis: ongoing, daily, and so on. If your child starts to exhibit somatic complaints (headaches, stomachaches) that seem geared to avoiding certain settings (i.e., school), then they may be experiencing bullying.

Your child may not outright have the words to say, "I am being bullied." However, if they report a high frequency of being teased, and they are reporting high levels of distress, you will be able to distinguish this yourself. Respond in much the same way you would for teasing; process feelings and discuss potential emotional/behavioral tools to help your child cope. In addition, you will likely need to get others involved: school personnel, other parents, those in charge of the setting where the bullying is happening, and so on. Advocate for protection of your child and appropriate interventions from the powers that be.

Teach your child that they never have to tolerate bullying. Repetitive, mean-spirited teasing is never okay, and you should encourage your child to speak up until it is resolved. Additionally, teach your child to disengage immediately should they start getting teased online, either by discontinuing contact with the cyberbully or by avoiding reading posts that are meant to be hurtful.

By law, public schools must provide transgender and gender-expansive students with a safe and affirming school environment. A critical element to meeting that obligation is by effectively addressing any bullying or harassment against a transgender or gender-expansive student. This includes harassment or bullying that is based on a student's gender presentation not matching gender stereotypes. As with other types of sex or gender discrimination, bullying and harassment against a transgender or gender-expansive student is covered by Title IX, a comprehensive federal law that prohibits discrimination on the basis of sex in any federally funded education program or activity. If your child reports being bullied, or describes interactions with peers that sound to you like bullying, find out about your school district's anti-bullying policies. Document the incidents in a journal or log and bring your concerns to school and district officials, in person and in writing. If you decide to go in person, consider sending a follow-up letter to the person or people you spoke with. This letter, which is a record of that meeting, should detail what was discussed and agreed upon. Ideally, you will be able to resolve the issue as a result of the meeting. If the school is not responsive to your concerns, you should contact an appropriate legal organization (see Appendix E for information about your options). You might need to file a complaint with a state or federal agency. (See Appendix E for more information on resources regarding bullying.)

WHY DO KIDS TEASE OR BULLY?

There are multiple reasons why kids tease. Sometimes they themselves have been teased and they either want to see what it feels like to be the perpetrator, or they are angry and hurting inside. Teasing can at times make other children feel powerful, which may certainly be sought after if a child is feeling powerless in one or more areas of their life. Teasing can be used as a way of impressing other kids, or making themselves seem more intimidating so that other kids might want to align themselves with them.

Young children are concrete and very "rule bound," meaning that they are focused on rules. Since the day a child begins exploring their world, they begin learning about rules, many of which are imposed by those raising them. This is how children learn about the world around them and learn how things work. Things fit into categories, which makes the world make sense. The more one is able to categorize something, the less thinking one has to do about it, and the less discomfort it triggers. When something doesn't follow the "rules" that a child has been taught, then there is discomfort and possible anxiety. Kids will work to have their world make sense again.

Many have been taught specific rules about gender: pink is for girls, boys don't cry, girls don't like sports, boys can't wear skirts, and so on. When a peer's gender expression doesn't fall in line with these "rules," kids can compulsively make it their job to let them know. It can be helpful to reflect with your child that not everyone yet understands there really are no rules when it comes to gender.

Additionally, because kids are essentially being controlled much of the time, teasing and bullying are likely an outlet for them to try to be the one to control someone else. Remind your child that peers are not in control of them; the adults at home and school are in charge of them, and they have said any way they are is okay.

Coaching Your Child

A conscious parent's task is to compassionately guide their child to grow into an aware, whole, happy person. Part of this guidance may sometimes involve shaping behavior by teaching skills of self-regulation, and using empathy to understand the impact of one's behavior on others. If your child exhibits a behavior that is negatively impacting others, and is a behavior they can change, coach them about this. Examples of this might be if they themselves are teasing peers, if they are physically aggressive, bossy in play, and so on.

It is important to remember that gender identity is not a behavior that is to be guided. Gender identity is simply a core characteristic of a person: whether they feel male, female, both, or neither. Likewise, gender expression is not a behavior that should be molded or changed to prevent teasing. If the gender expression of your child is a reflection of who they are, then it is not a behavior they can change. Teach your child instead how to care for themselves in response to behaviors from others.

This bears repeating: Being gender-expansive is not a behavior; it is a way a person *is*. The conscious parent wants to embrace and accept their child "as is," with no strings attached. Informing a child about possible teasing that may come from displaying a core characteristic (something the child cannot change) has the potential to complicate your child's ability to listen to their inner voice. Since your child cannot change being gender-expansive or transgender, what may result is an inhibition of expression or an anxiety regarding how they authentically are. Again, this is not about a minor social infraction that a child can learn how to avoid. This is about your child being who they are, and they are doing absolutely nothing wrong.

AVOID WARNING YOUR CHILD

Letting your child choose behaviors while informing them of possible ramifications is a parenting basic. As a conscious parent, you want to allow your child to listen to their inner voice and make decisions based on their own internal sense of what is right. Nonetheless, you may still find yourself "warning" them about possible outcomes to the various choices at hand. In fact, it may seem like the compassionate thing to do.

Describing possible social outcomes to a child's gender expansiveness is often something parents do so that their child is prepared for potential responses so as not to be surprised or hurt by them. However, doing this does not teach them first and foremost to listen to their inner voice. This is teaching them to always consider external factors, in addition to listening to their inner voice. Your child's inner voice can get muffled if they place too much consideration on possible external reactions.

"Warning" your child that dressing a certain way or engaging in certain preferences could result in getting teased may not have the protective effect you are aiming for. Not only does this enforce gender stereotypes but it may also teach your child to prescribe to what others say is the best way for them to be. Much like you wouldn't "warn" a child about being teased for wearing an oxygen tank to combat oxygen deprivation, try not to warn your gender-expansive child to avoid their natural gender expression. Living their natural gender expression is their way of expressing their authentic self. This is not something to be stifled or modified just so others will approve.

Most parents are coming from a very loving place when they explain to their child what may lay ahead. However, this can instill fear and dread in the place of blissful innocence. When you teach your child to anticipate a negative outcome, you are not teaching them to stay in the present moment. You are teaching them to bring anxiety from possible future moments, and have that possible future play a part in the here and now (either by creating negative feelings or by causing the child to somehow modify their behavior/expression).

Moreover, these "warnings" may make your child less equipped to deal with the teasing that could come with being gender-expansive. They might become fearful to let their true preferences show, even though those expressions are reflective of something they can't change. They may look at everyone they meet with just a little bit of suspicion or mistrust. This does not contribute to an open, confident way of relating to the world. Children come across negative peer responses and become inhibited soon enough. As a parent you want to work against that process, not assist it.

Supporting and Empowering

Instead of warning your child, empower them. Parents can help their child by unconditionally supporting who they are on the inside so they know without a doubt they are important, they are valued, and they are okay exactly as they are. This won't prevent the pain associated with teasing, but it will help build the internalized, stable ego strength in the child so that they understand their basic worth doesn't change based on what others say. Here are some ways you can empower your child:

- **Stay connected.** Ask the best and worst parts of day at bedtime or dinnertime. If your child seems to clam up under one-on-one questioning, ask questions in the car. With your eyes on the road and not on them, some children tend to open up more.

- **If your child reports teasing, ask questions and fight the impulse to just give "answers."** You will find out a lot more about your child's feelings and ability to handle the teasing if you avoid jumping in and trying to fix the situation.

- **If your child asks if you think they may be teased, ask more questions.** "What do you think?" If they also want to hear what you think, be honest. You can say something like, "Maybe, because some kids may think there are rules about what other kids should wear." Model confidence that even if you do think teasing is a possibility, your child can handle it. (If you are nervous about the potential of your child being teased for an interest, toy, clothing choice, and so on, don't show it.)

○ **Model appropriate responses to others if they question or mock your child's gender expression or presentation of gender identity.** Be it in response to a family friend or a stranger at the grocery store, don't apologize for your child's behavior or gender expression. Own it, so your child can, too.

BUILDING SELF-CONFIDENCE

Supporting your child's true self at home facilitates the establishment of a strong core foundation of self-esteem and self-confidence. Teach your child, "I am awesome just the way I am," until they believe it and it is a part of their core self. (This is important for *all* kids, not just gender-expansive kids.) You want to help your child create a stable sense of contentedness and peace, one that is not easily disrupted by the actions of others. This begins with a sturdy connection to one's inner self, and the ability to trust one's internal sense of truth. If your child's internal voice tells them they are inherently good, and that they are accepted as they are, messages about the opposite will not feel true. This makes it easier for your child to stay separate from the negative and helps them more easily connect to the positive.

Equipping Your Child

If your child comes home and reports being teased, ask questions; you don't have to be the one with all the answers. This will help you get a feel for how much understanding your child has about the reasons behind the teasing. "Why do you think they teased you about wearing a skirt?" or "Why do you think they said that?"

This is a great time to teach your child about theory of mind, which is the ability to understand that other people have their own thoughts, beliefs, and motivations that are separate from your own and may influence not only their behavior but also their ability to understand you. (Children with an autism spectrum disorder may struggle with theory of mind, thereby making it more difficult for them to infer or understand the motivations of others.) Discuss and practice possible responses based on the teasing so that your child can feel more equipped should it happen again.

At dinnertime, bedtime, or some other appropriate time ask your child about the best and worst parts of their day. If they report teasing, process it with them. Talk with them about how it made them feel, and how they can take care of themselves when they have that feeling.

TEASING TOOLBOX

Help your child create a toolbox of responses (both verbal and behavioral) to deal with teasing. You can write down these responses and put them in an actual box your child can revisit from time to time. Or, you can make a list with your child that you can both review often.

Verbal responses are best used with children your child considers to be friends: "That hurts my feelings," "Please don't say that," "Please stop," and so on. However, saying these verbal responses to children who are not your child's friend, or who are mean to your child on a consistent basis, may open your child up to more teasing.

Practice assertiveness skills with your child. Teach your child to look strong by lifting their chin up, making eye contact, and putting their shoulders back. They should face the person they are talking to and use a firm but kind voice.

The first incident of teasing is usually a test; help your child to pass the test. Explain the importance of acting like the teasing doesn't bother them. If another child senses the teasing has upset your child, it may fuel the fire. Teach your child to hold back emotion until they are in a safe place or speaking to an adult they trust. Also discuss the importance of not fighting back with their own mean words. Here are some other points for your child to keep in mind:

- **Ignore.** Act as though the other child is invisible. Can't see them, can't hear them. Make sure your child understands this may temporarily make the teaser's behavior worse before it stops. Commit to the ignoring and stick to it.

- **Walk away.** Move to another area. Join another group of kids or a kid who is typically friendly.

- **Stay within adult eyesight or earshot.** Kids aren't going to relentlessly tease or bully other kids who are near an adult. Talk with your child about what it might look like to subtly move within range of an adult.

- **Get adult help.** If the teasing is getting to your child, if your child is having difficulty ignoring it, or if your child is in physical danger, teach your child to get adult help right away. Explain the importance of saying, "I need help because . . ." as opposed to "telling on" a peer. Discuss the tone your child should use when assertively asking for help.

- **Role play.** If your child reports being teased, practice responses at home. Have your child tease you while you model appropriate responses, then switch.

RESPOND VERSUS REACT

If your child comes home and reports being teased, you may have a very strong emotional response. It is essential for your child that you monitor your internal process and focus on responding rather than reacting. If you react, your unconscious mind may take charge. Your unconscious mind will flood you with fear, anxiety, and pain for your child. You may unintentionally project these feelings onto your child. Also, your child may avoid telling you about being teased if they know it upsets you.

> If your child comes home and is sad or upset about teasing they encountered, do your best to act like it's not upsetting to you. You can show compassion for your child without showing that it is hurting you.

Responding, unlike reacting, will come from a place of conscious awareness. You will be mindful of your own emotional response but will not let it rule your behavior. You will be able to remind yourself of your child's emotional sovereignty; you will be mindful that your child may not be feeling exactly as you are feeling. Because your role is to help your child cope with their own unique feelings about the situation, it is important that you do not allow yourself to be washed over by your own emotions. Validate the feelings your child has, talk about coping skills, and remind them of how wonderful they are. Last but not least, take care of yourself and your own feelings!

Important Points to Consider

Listening about your child being teased can be a very hard thing for a parent to take. Talk to your friends, talk to other parents, talk to a therapist. Remind yourself this is not something you can "fix" or prevent, but also remind yourself that you are doing right by your gender-expansive child by nurturing their true self. Here are some other points to keep in mind:

○ It is important for you to assess if your child is being teased or bullied, for any reason. Keep open communication, ask open-ended questions, ask your child about the best and worst parts of their day, ask intermittently if anyone has said anything to hurt their feelings, and so on.

O If you sense your child is being bullied, intervene until it is resolved.

O Instead of warning your child to make changes to avoid getting teased, equip and empower your child with self-confidence, self-esteem, and coping skills.

O If your child reports being teased, remain separate enough to help them cope and prepare. If they sense you can't handle it, they will have little faith in their ability to handle it themselves.

CHAPTER 13

School

Unless you homeschool your child, the school they attend will likely be the place where they spend the most time outside of the home. It can be difficult to send your child into an environment where you are not sure how "conscious" the approach will be. You may wonder how much your child will be allowed to develop their own sense of self within the structured environment, or if your child's voice will be heard among the many. If you are parenting a gender-expansive child, you will likely have concerns about how the school and classroom environment will impact their feelings about their gender expression or gender identity, or how others will respond to these things. This chapter covers the ways you can help set your child up for success in the school environment.

Advocating for Your Child

At one point or another in the educational journey, most parents will have to advocate for their child's needs. As a parent, you have the unique viewpoint of knowing your child's temperament and personality, their personal history, and how the academic and social environment of school impacts them.

For the gender-expansive child, specific advocacy will need to be done to facilitate a gender-affirmative environment at school. You may also need to get involved to make sure the school is doing its part to protect your child from bullying, embracing your child for who they are, and setting them up for the best possible academic success.

Ask your child's school for a copy of its nondiscrimination policy. If there is nothing in the policy about gender expression or identity, ask them to write it in.

ADVOCATING FOR YOUR GENDER-EXPANSIVE CHILD

If your child is gender-expansive, it may be best to meet with the principal and teacher to see how supportive/gender affirmative the school is going to be for your child. Share your thoughts and your gender-affirming approach with them. Let them know what you expect as far as how adults and other kids should respond to your child. You will get a feeling for how comfortable these professionals seem to be with children who do not conform to the expectations of their assigned gender. Get a sense for their approach; do they seem to wish to minimize the distractions that your gender-expansive child could present? Or do they seem determined to minimize any distress or discomfort that your child may experience as a result of expressing themselves authentically?

ADVOCATING FOR TRANSITION

If your child is transitioning in the middle of the school year, or starting a new school year at the school they attended before transition, advocate for the administration to handle it the way you think is best. Talk to the principal about specific policies in place to protect your child, provide resources, and ask about teacher/staff training. A great resource is "Schools in Transition: A Guide for Supporting Transgender Students in K–12 Schools" by Gender Spectrum. Ask how the transition will be communicated to your child's classmates and the rest of the children/staff who interact with your child. Decide (in partnership with your child) whether or not you think they should be present for the announcement. Help the teacher with the wording so your child is most comfortable, and most accurately represented. If your child identifies on the binary, you may want to give the teacher the words to use, such as "heart and brain of a boy" or "heart and brain of a girl." If your child is nonbinary, perhaps a drawing of a spectrum of gender identity can help the teacher explain this concept to your child's peers.

Encourage the teacher and other staff to use your child's new name (if changing) and new pronouns purposefully and regularly so that your child's peers hear them and know that this language is expected of them as well.

ADVOCATING FOR YOUR TRANSGENDER CHILD

If your child is transgender, get familiar with any existing laws (state and federal) that protect your child and allow them to participate in sports activities and use facilities in line with their gender identity. Please see Appendix E for specific school resources.

> You will need to advocate for your child so that they feel most comfortable at school, and can be most supported to learn. This advocacy varies depending on the child's age, stage of transition, level of disclosure, and personal comfort level.

You may need to advocate for which bathroom is safest and most comfortable for them to use, certain aspects of participating in physical education, and for the name and gender marker that is listed in the school's system. If a child's transgender status is undisclosed to other students, having a substitute call out their birth name can be extremely distressing and most certainly takes away from their ability to focus on academics. If your child's birth name is listed in the school's online program, then using that name to log in can be distracting at best, and extremely upsetting at worst. This is an unnecessary stressor for your child, and issues of proper name use in school software systems are worth advocating for until they are resolved. Insist that your child's name be changed to their new one.

The Gender Climate

Perhaps even more important than how the school is willing to respond to your specific child is how the overall gender climate is at the school. Is it welcoming to diversity? Does it have a rigidly engrained "gender role" structure that will make those who do not fit into it uncomfortable? Is unique self-expression encouraged or discouraged? Do there seem to be conservative ways of viewing those who do not fit into the mainstream, and is there pressure to conform? In extreme cases, you may decide this type of school environment is not right for your child and you may opt to not enroll them in it. If the climate does not seem as progressive as you would like but they seem willing to learn and change, try to connect them with organizations that can provide education and training in regard to gender diversity.

The school policies and administration all play a role in communicating how the school as a whole feels about issues such as gender creativity. The students pick up on this and will act accordingly. Will they feel compelled to uphold gender norms that are in place from either implicit or explicit explanation? Or are diversity and acceptance the standard?

GENDER LESSON

The following lesson was created for teachers who have gender-expansive children in their classrooms. However, to change society's stereotypes, reduce stigmatization of gender expansiveness, decrease bullying, and increase acceptance, this lesson would be helpful to incorporate in all classrooms. As a parent, you can ask to present the lesson to the class or ask for the teacher to do it.

This lesson is to be presented at the very beginning of the school year so as to set standards of expectations for behavior, and it can be reviewed as needed throughout the school year. It was created for Grades K–5, though it can be modified as needed. Role-play prompts are included at the end of the lesson for comprehension reinforcement. Give the child a scenario and have them attempt a positive response first; give suggestions as needed. Lastly, the teacher should post the "In Our Classroom" rules (see Appendix F) as a reminder of the acceptance that is expected.

Lesson to Be Presented to Students

For a very long time, people have been separating things into what girls like and what boys like. A lot of people think these things are very different, and call them "boy things" and "girl things." Have *you* noticed that?

What are some things some people might say are "girl things" or "boy things"? What might some people say are "girl toys" and "boy toys"?

The truth is, all children get to pick what they like, and everyone likes different things. Repeat after me: There is no such thing as a "boy thing" or a "girl thing." Some kids are boys who like things that other people think are for girls. Some kids are girls who like things that other people think are for boys. It can hurt their feelings if you or someone else says something to them about it, or act like there are rules about how someone should be. That would be like saying only girls can eat ice cream, and only boys can eat jelly beans! That would just be silly! Sweets and treats are to be enjoyed by everyone, just like most things in life.

Are there certain colors that some people think only girls like and colors that only boys like? Most people think girls like pink and purple, which is okay, but it's silly to think that *only* girls like pink and purple, or that girls *only* like pink and purple! There are plenty of boys out there who like pink and purple, too, and lots of girls who don't. Lots of people think only boys can like blue! Girls can like blue, too. All the colors of the rainbow are for everyone, and it's fun that we all get to pick our favorite. You don't want anyone telling *you* what your favorite color should be, do you?

Some people also have very strong ideas about how kids of certain genders should look and dress. Is it okay for some girls to have short hair, and some boys to have long hair? Of course it is! How someone chooses to dress is up to them, too. Some girls wear skirts and dresses, and some girls wear shorts and pants. Some boys wear shorts and pants, and some boys wear skirts and dresses. This may surprise some people, but it certainly isn't wrong.

How someone dresses and wears their hair is a part of their "style." Everyone's style is different. What if everyone were to dress and look exactly alike? That would probably be very boring! The next time you see someone who wears their hair a little different than you expected or is wearing something that surprises you, be kind and say, "I like your style."

How wonderful would it be to have a classroom (or a *world*) where kids just get to like what they like? Are you ready to help create a world like that?

One of the most important things to remember is to be kind to one another. Ask yourself how you would feel if you were the other person. Be sure to avoid saying anything that would hurt someone else's feelings. If you can see another kid likes something, don't tell them why they shouldn't. Remind yourself, "different people like different things," "it's okay to be different," and "I am accepting of others."

If you hear someone telling another kid there are rules about how to play, how to be, or how to dress, stand up for them! Remember, you are helping create a world that is more accepting. Nicely tell the other person what you have learned from this lesson. You can say something like this:

- "That's their style, and I like it."
- "Anyone can play with anything."
- "Everyone is different. Different people like different things."
- "Please don't tease my friend. I like them just the way they are."

Remember these important points:

- There is no such thing as a "boy thing" or "girl thing."
- All toys are for all children.
- Colors are for everyone.
- People are different and everyone likes different things.
- Everyone gets to pick how they wear their hair.
- Everyone gets to pick the way they dress.
- Everyone gets to pick their own style.
- Being accepting of others is cool.

Role Plays

Act out the best way to handle the following situations:

- You are playing house and a girl wants to be the dad.
- You hear someone teasing a boy about wearing a skirt.
- A group of boys playing soccer tells a girl, "You can't play! No girls allowed!"
- You're having a tea party and a boy wants to join in.
- You see a girl getting teased for having short hair.
- You see a boy wearing a pink backpack.

Legalities and Other Logistics to Consider

From the very start, attempt to develop a collaborative relationship with the school administration. Be careful not to push them away, especially in your first contacts, even though those initial conversations and meetings may be frustrating. The school may have limited experience in working with gender-expansive/transgender youth and may therefore say and do things that seem largely ignorant to you. Visualize yourself joining forces with the administration to make a stronger team for your child, rather than two opposing teams. The administration at your child's school may end up playing a huge role in your child's life. Joining forces with them, and patiently advocating/educating for your child, increases the chance that your child will have a positive school experience. This type of relationship also ensures that school administrators will be more willing to work with you if you need to address your child's other educational needs or those of your other children.

The laws are different in every state, so you will need to familiarize yourself with your state's laws that are pertinent to your child. Some states have very specific laws to protect transgender students. These laws outline their rights to use facilities and participate in sports teams that are in line with their gender identities.

Some states simply extend existing anti-discrimination laws to include gender identity, which a court or state agency can then interpret to include those specific rights.

There are a number of federal laws that protect transgender and gender-expansive students in school. Title IX is a federal law that bans sex discrimination in schools that receive federal funds. Although the law does not use the words "gender expression/identity," the legal definition of sex includes both gender identity and gender expression, meaning that it covers transgender and gender-expansive students. The federal government has interpreted Title IX to prohibit schools from excluding transgender students from the sex-separated facilities that match their gender identity, and it requires schools to properly address bullying and harassment based on a student's gender identity or expression.

Transgender and gender-expansive students are also protected by various provisions of the U.S. Constitution. One example is the Equal Protection Clause, which guarantees all people "equal protection of the laws." Thus, no matter how the school administration feels about issues related to the LGBT community, they cannot single out LGBT students or treat them differently than other students because of their sexual orientation or gender identity. The First Amendment, which protects freedom of expression, is another example of an important constitutional protection for gender-expansive and transgender youth. Schools must allow transgender or gender-expansive youth to dress in a manner consistent with their gender identity, so long as they follow the dress codes that apply to all students.

Another important law that protects transgender youth is the Family Education Rights and Privacy Act, or FERPA. This law prohibits schools from sharing personally identifiable information about your child with others, including other teachers and school personnel. You can also use the law to challenge the accuracy of your child's school records. Although the school is not required to correct the record, if the school denies your request, it must at least provide you with an opportunity to write a note that explains the inaccuracy. That note will accompany the student's records. Some parents have been successful in changing their child's gender marker on school records prior to a legal gender marker change.

To help improve their school climate, many transgender and gender-expansive youth are interested in joining or starting a Gay-Straight Alliance (GSA) or similar group. A federal law called the Equal Access Act prohibits a school from placing additional requirements or restrictions on those types of student groups. For example, the school cannot ask the students forming a GSA to create bylaws before allowing the group to form, if the school does not require that of all noncurricular student groups.

If you feel your child is being mistreated at school, talk to school officials first and district officials if necessary. You should document your conversations with school and district personnel, either by e-mail or letter. In addition to creating a paper trail of your contact with the district, you should also be documenting how the mistreatment is affecting your child. If your child is old enough, they should keep a log or journal that documents what is happening to them at school and how it makes them feel. This can be very helpful in demonstrating to the school the severity of the problem. Documenting your child's experience in this way can also help your case should you later decide to file a complaint or lawsuit against the school.

In the event that you are not able to resolve the issue at the school level and are contemplating pursuing the issue further, you should contact appropriate legal resources (see Appendix E for a list of organizations that can provide assistance). Depending on your specific circumstances and the laws of your state, there may be a number of options you can pursue. You may want to seek legal advice to determine which are most appropriate for your child and your family.

Please note that much of this information pertains only to public schools and those schools that receive government funding. Private schools are not typically required to follow the same set of rules as public schools, but that does not necessarily mean that your child has no legal protections.

If your child attends a nonpublic school, or a school that does not receive government funding, you should still first attempt to collaborate with the school to support your child's needs, just like you would with a public school. If this does not work you can seek outside assistance to pursue a remedy. Keep in mind that your legal options with a nonpublic school are likely going to be more limited as compared to a public school.

Please see Appendix E for more resources to help with your child's rights in school.

NAMES/GENDER MARKERS

School administration tends to have a knee-jerk response to requests for changing a child's name and gender in the district's student information system. They will typically tell parents this can only be done after a court-ordered name and gender change. Depending on the laws in your state, however, the school may only be legally required to keep your child's legal birth name and gender marker somewhere in the permanent file, but they can change everything else to your child's affirmed name and gender before a legal change. The district can change your child's official record to reflect your child's chosen name and correct gender once you have obtained a court order changing that information.

If the school is required to use your child's birth name on school documents such as Individualized Education Programs or standardized testing, the school needs to implement practices that safeguard the confidentiality of your child's birth name and gender. You will likely need to advocate for this safeguard and be very clear if there is an issue of privacy surrounding this for your child.

Again, even if your child has not obtained a court-ordered name and gender change, your child still has the right to be addressed by the name and pronoun that corresponds to their gender identity. A court-ordered name or gender change is not required, and official records do not need to be changed before your child is known solely by their chosen name at school. In some states, people may change their name through "common law name change" by using the name in everyday interactions for an extended period of time.

Once your child has socially transitioned and you feel confident about legally changing their name and gender, doing so can make navigating the school system (and other systems such as air travel) much easier. If you are interested in pursuing the legal name and gender change, see your state or county's court website for requirements and needed documentation.

Important Points to Consider

While it may sometimes seem like you don't have much control over the school and how they operate, you can play a pivotal role in shaping your child's school environment by advocating for affirmation and inclusion. It will be beneficial to your child to know that you are there to stand up for them when needed. You can also do some "behind the scenes" work to ensure a good school environment for your child, about which your child might not be aware.

O Whether your child is gender-expansive or transgender, you will likely find yourself in the role of educating and advocating. This advocacy may include having conversations with personnel who have some influence over your child's environment or working to enhance nondiscrimination policies.

O Don't assume an answer you get from a school is based on actual policy. Continue to advocate for what you know is best for your child, and bring in outside help as needed.

O There is a huge emphasis on education in society today, but remember that it is but one aspect of your child. Your child's sense of self, and self-worth, take priority over academics and education. Make decisions about your child's schooling based on this order of importance.

 **CHAPTER 14**

Dysphoria

Dysphoria associated with one's gender identity, for the purposes of this book, is the discomfort and depression that comes from having a body that is incongruent with one's gender identity, or from not being read as and treated as the gender one is inside. Dysphoria can range from unpleasant to life-threatening. It will be important for you, as the parent of a gender-expansive child, to find out if your child experiences gender dysphoria, and if so, to what extent. This chapter will discuss the basics of dysphoria as well as some of the signs and symptoms so that you can be better equipped to help your child.

Body Dysphoria

Just as everyone's gender identity is different, so is a transgender person's relationship with their body. Not every transgender child, adolescent, or adult has the same journey or experience when it comes to body dysphoria. Some transgender individuals don't have body dysphoria at all. They accept their body as is, with little desire to change it. Some start out with a little dysphoria that intensifies over time. Still others start out with intense dysphoria that eases as the years go on. Some don't have body dysphoria until certain developmental stages, including puberty or the emergence of the interest in dating.

Some parents look to how their child feels about their body as an indicator of whether or not they are transgender. This may not be a good gauge, as young children in particular don't typically have much body dysphoria. They tend to approach their bodies with a type of universal acceptance, usually the type that comes along with low inhibitions and childhood innocence, including a lack of over-analyzing the way things are. For these kids, social dysphoria may be more of a concern that is largely alleviated by social transition.

However, some young children do have an inherent sense of what they think their bodies "should" look like, based on concrete associations with their authentic gender. They may ask when they will get the body parts associated with their authentic gender, or why they don't have them in the first place. Again, ask questions to find out existing assumptions before answering these questions. Your child may also desire to have the same body parts as the parent or siblings with whom they identify gender-wise. Validate these thoughts and feelings. You do not need to "fix" the feelings or make them go away; you simply need to listen and let your child know you empathize with how they feel.

Some parents wonder when it is the appropriate time to discuss medical interventions or possible surgical interventions when their child is expressing body dysphoria. Honesty and transparency, based on your child's developmental level, is usually best. You do not need to volunteer a lot of information as soon as your child expresses body dysphoria. However, if they are asking specific questions or expressing distress/hopelessness about what they think the future holds for them body-wise, feel free to fill them in. Start with minimal details and work up as your child inquires. Some children find great relief in knowing there are medical interventions that will prevent certain changes, as well as other interventions that may eventually help them feel more aligned with their bodies.

Sometimes, incongruence between one's mind and body can contribute to thoughts and feelings of having the "wrong" body. This is where you, the conscious parent, come in. While allowing space for your child to have feelings about their body, gently guide them to choose language that empowers and celebrates themselves. Using the word "wrong" to describe their body can create a disconnect that is not healthy. Instead, give your child words that focus on the positive aspects of their body. If your child's body is healthy, help them focus on that. Assist your child in identifying all the many things their body can do or help them do. Have them name things they like about their bodies. If they struggle, give them some things *you* like about their body. For example: "your beating heart," "your sparkling eyes," "your happy smile," "your arms that hug," and so on.

While using the terms "girl bodies" and "boy bodies" with a different gender in the brain and heart can help children understand the concept of being transgender, eventually you will want to move away from these terms. It will be important for your child to understand that their body belongs to them and their authentic gender. For example, if they are a boy in their heart and brain, they are a boy, and therefore have a boy's body. It may be different than other boys' bodies, but it is a boy's body nonetheless.

Social Dysphoria

If body dysphoria is the distress one gets from looking in the mirror and having it not reflect one's authentic self, social dysphoria is the incongruent reflection of self in the mirror of society. Society, in this definition, includes everyone from those out and about in the general public to loved ones. Anyone within an individual's environment can create social dysphoria. This can occur in a number of different ways including but not limited to:

○ Misgendering or miscategorizing the individual by gender based on appearance.

○ Making comments about the transgender individual's appearance that is not in line with their authentic gender identity.

○ Using pronouns and names that are not reflective of a person's gender identity.

Social dysphoria can make a person engage in avoidance behaviors when it comes to being around people who do not read them as their true gender. Social transition often helps with this immensely. If your child continues to be misread after social transition, you may need to be proactive by using pronouns and name purposefully when around others to clear up any confusion. This may help your child relax and know that those other people are not confused about their true gender and are not misreading them.

Don't Poke the Dysphoria Monster

For transgender kids, adolescents, and even adults, a Dysphoria Monster may be lurking nearby. In order to facilitate children's understanding of addiction, the metaphor of the "Addiction Monster" can be helpful. This metaphor creates an image that can help children understand when someone is struggling with addiction. It goes like this: When someone has an addiction, they have an addiction monster with them that is sometimes small and manageable, sometimes huge and overpowering, but never nonexistent. When the monster is huge, it has them in their grip, throwing them around, banging them up, holding them hostage. When the addiction becomes more under control, the individual may have more power over the monster, like walking it on a leash. After some time of sobriety when the urges have decreased dramatically and the individual is in recovery, the monster may get small enough to tuck away in their pocket. But, it's always there, and the person needs to take care to keep it small.

Transgender kids and parents of transgender kids can understand dysphoria in much the same way if they conjure the metaphorical Dysphoria Monster. Most transgender people experience and relate to dysphoria differently. Some have very little dysphoria (a tiny monster tucked in their pocket), while some have debilitating dysphoria (picture the gender dysphoria equivalent of Godzilla). Dysphoria can fluctuate on an hourly, daily, weekly basis. How much dysphoria is present on a day-to-day basis can be dependent on temperament, life experience, support, stage of transition, relationship status, triggers, and much more.

Here is an example of how the Dysphoria Monster can work: Picture a transmasculine adult walking down the street with a female friend. He's feeling good, confident, content, and enjoying the day. His Dysphoria Monster is quiet and he doesn't really notice it. Suddenly he and his friend enter a restaurant and they are greeted with, "Hello, ladies." His monster is awakened! Suddenly it is growling and breathing down his neck. The monster sits with them at the table for the rest of the meal as he agonizes over being misgendered.

Ever heard of the expression "don't poke the bear"? It's important as the parent of a transgender child that you "don't poke the Dysphoria Monster." Be aware that this monster is lurking nearby and that it is in your child's best interest that the monster stays docile. Unfortunately, parents can fairly easily poke the monster because they are usually the ones who are around the child the most. This can happen in any number of ways: misgendering (using wrong pronouns), using their birth name, commenting on body parts, commenting on appearance, giving tips on how to be masculine/feminine, and the list goes on. Many of these things can be unintentional and may be hard to avoid, especially as you are getting used to your child's transition. Other ways of poking the monster can be avoided. Tips about how to better present as one's affirmed gender may be offered lovingly and yet be taken in a hurtful manner. Additionally, it may be helpful for you to remember there is no one way to be a certain gender. While encouraging your child to act a certain way to assert their gender identity, you may accidentally decrease their self-confidence, increase their self-doubt, and reinforce gender stereotypes.

Empathizing with your child will help you to know what may trigger dysphoria. If you know your child is unhappy with certain parts of their body, avoid talking about them and check in with your child later if they have to be discussed for any reason. Try to comprehend and empathize with how it might feel to be incongruent with one's body and/or be misread in society. This will help you connect with the core feelings of dysphoria that your child might be experiencing.

Siblings may be guilty of poking the Dysphoria Monster. Siblings usually know exactly what buttons to push to upset each other. Make it clear with your gender-expansive child's siblings that assigned sex, gender identity, expression, transition, and the like are off-limits when it comes to teasing or handling conflict.

Do you want to know how big and unruly your child's Dysphoria Monster currently is, and how to avoid inadvertently awakening it? Here are some tips:

O Educate yourself on dysphoria. Attempt to understand the degrees of dysphoria and how they can affect your child specifically.

O Check in. For younger children, you can ask specific questions such as, "How are you feeling about your body?" or "How are you feeling about how others see you?" For the older child or preteen, don't be afraid to ask, "How's your dysphoria?" (or whatever word they would like you to use). Usually they will know exactly what you mean, and you will get the most direct answer that way.

- Ask your child what triggers their dysphoria the most. This will help you not only learn to avoid causing these triggers yourself, but also will alert you to check in after you witness one of these triggers happening.

- Ask your child what helps lower their dysphoria. Ask when they feel the least dysphoric, and then try to increase or replicate these experiences and situations.

Overlap with Anxiety/Depression

Dysphoria often causes anxiety and/or depression, although not always. Symptoms of anxiety or depression associated with dysphoria can be fleeting, circumstantial, or relatively stable. At times, it is difficult to glean what is caused by dysphoria and what is not. The individual may be experiencing dysphoria *and* symptoms of depression and anxiety, which are their own separate entities. One way to distinguish what is associated with dysphoria is to see if the anxiety and depression are alleviated by things like social transition or gender affirmation.

> If the child is being seen and acknowledged for how they feel on the inside, but continues to display concerning mood disruptions, then these disruptions may be independent of the dysphoria. This does not mean the mood disruptions need to be addressed prior to addressing your child's gender; it simply means they need to be addressed in conjunction with gender.

Your child may not experience as much improvement in their anxiety and depression with transition as other dysphoric children and youth might experience. Along with gender-affirming interventions, your child may benefit from therapeutic interventions such as talk/play therapy and cognitive behavioral therapy (CBT). If such therapies do not improve your child's anxiety and/or depression, medication may need to be considered.

The transgender population has historically had a much higher rate of self-harm and suicide attempts than the general population. Family and societal support and affirmation are significant protective factors, but they are not the only factors. A person's temperament, inherent resiliency, self-esteem, and ability to tolerate dysphoria/challenges of transition all may play a role. Additionally, mood disruptions that exist outside of dysphoria can exacerbate distress or even negate one's ability to cope with distress. As a child gets older and their peer group becomes more important, bullying and other forms of peer rejection seem to be major risk factors.

If your child is expressing distress and/or dysphoria, connect them with other transgender children or teens. Spending time with peers they can relate to can be extremely relieving to transgender youth. You may be able to find groups in your area through your child's therapist or online.

Information about dysphoria, depression, and self-harm can be very scary for parents of transgender kids. In order to keep fear from controlling you, stay in the now. Check in with your child often, and don't ever be afraid to ask about their level of dysphoria, thoughts of self-harm, or thoughts of suicide. If thoughts of self-harm are revealed, get your child immediate help from a mental health provider, preferably a therapist who is gender-affirming.

Talk with your child's therapist about safety planning, and come up with a safety plan with your child. If you are ever concerned about their immediate safety, you can have them assessed for hospitalization at the nearest emergency room.

Autism and Gender Dysphoria

There does seem to be some overlap with autism and gender dysphoria, the etiology of which is currently unknown. Just as gender exists on a spectrum, so too does autism, making the possibilities of interplay between each spectrum practically limitless. Knowing why autism and gender dysphoria tend to co-occur is not necessary in terms of supporting where your child lands on each spectrum and custom-tailoring your conscious responses based on your child's needs. Additionally, there is much more to your child's whole self than their gender and/or where they land on the autism spectrum.

Parents of an autistic child who is also displaying gender expansiveness may question their child's ability to accurately communicate how they feel. These parents also may wonder if the gender expansiveness is tied to, or perhaps a symptom of, their child's autism. Autistic children can exhibit repetitive behavior and have a fairly restricted set of interests, and may become hyperfocused on those interests. It may seem at times that the gender expression or preferences are simply a manifestation of this aspect of their child's autism.

However, one may argue that given the special characteristics of children with autism, the information you receive about their gender may be more pure and uninhibited than if it came from a child who is more careful about their presentation based on social pressures. Since an autism spectrum disorder (ASD) affects an individual's ability to socially communicate (the degree to which varies depending on the child and place on spectrum), and gender dysphoria is often highly impacted by social pressures, parents of an autistic child may see the gender dysphoria being exhibited differently as compared to a child without autism. A child with autism may be less inhibited, and therefore somewhat more authentic, about their true gender expression and/or identity because they will be less worried about how it impacts others or how others think of them. However, they may have difficulty explaining or describing their gender journey given they may struggle with knowing how to give others insight into how they might be feeling. They may assume others already know, or making others understand may not be very important to them.

Other factors that may affect an autistic gender-expansive child's gender expression and ability to understand/communicate their true gender include but are not limited to: co-occurring health problems, sensory processing difficulties, sensitivities to medication, and unique communication patterns. These factors do not preclude the ability for an autistic child to "know" their gender, but they may affect the journey. Autistic children who feel more genderqueer than binary might need some help in processing this, as they tend to have more "black and white" thinking, as well as difficulty with ambiguity.

In no uncertain terms, parents of children with autism should feel empowered to be gender affirming, and they should rest assured their children have the ability to know their gender just as every other child does. Children with an autism spectrum disorder and who are gender-expansive likely have much to offer and many strengths that will help them on this journey. Additionally, these elements of your child may open up your heart and your mind more than you could have imagined possible.

Important Points to Consider

Dysphoria is a sense of unease or discomfort with one's body or way of being perceived in society regarding their gender, and can take on many forms. Become familiar not only with the concept but also with your child's personal experience with dysphoria. With support and gender affirmation, many youth and adults report a decrease of dysphoria over time.

O Everyone experiences body dysphoria differently, and some not at all.

O Social dysphoria is connected to how one is perceived in society and by those who love them. Social transition can ease this, but remnants may remain if people in your child's life continue to misgender them or misunderstand them.

O Interact with your child in a way that keeps dysphoria in your conscious awareness, but work in partnership with your child to keep the Dysphoria Monster at bay. This doesn't mean walking on eggshells; rather, it means you should be aware of statements or situations that both increase and decrease your child's dysphoria.

○ If affirming and supporting your child's gender doesn't ease their symptoms of anxiety and depression much, your child may be struggling with mood disruptions that are separate from the gender dysphoria. Make sure your child is getting these symptoms addressed, which will make them feel better equipped to cope with challenges and will improve their quality of life.

○ Many children are on both the autism and gender spectrums, creating a uniquely beautiful gender presentation. Children with ASD are just as capable of knowing their gender as any other child, and may be able to more simplistically express their "true" gender identities.

CHAPTER 15

Coping and Self-Care

If you're on an airplane with your child and the pressure drops causing the oxygen masks to release, whose face are you supposed to put it on first? That's right, yours. This may go against your internal parenting instincts because, as a parent, you are typically looking to take care of your children before yourself. However, if you place the oxygen mask on your child and then pass out, your child no longer has a caretaker. Even worse, they are now in charge of taking care of you. This is a uniquely distressing situation for a child. This is a valuable analogy that drives home the importance of taking care of yourself in order to take care of your child: You don't want your child in that position in this airplane scenario, or in everyday life situations. Your child needs to know that you can care for both them and yourself.

Coping

Coping is more than just "dealing with" something. Coping is doing okay *while* dealing with something. It's important for you to build your arsenal of coping skills so that you can call upon them when necessary. Here are some suggestions to help build your arsenal:

- **Look for humor in everyday situations.** When you are able to laugh you are able to see the joy and connectedness of things. Laughing helps you downplay the sensation that everything feels disconnected and purposeless. Laughing can stave off anxiety, and laughing with someone can join you together.

- **Know what activities raise your spirits and engage in them when the going gets tough.** Whether it's getting outside and connecting with nature or visiting with a good friend, keep a list of these activities nearby and do them when needed.

- **Be flexible.** Flexibility is a key part of becoming a more conscious human being. It allows you to be open to new opportunities and doesn't allow you to get too attached to a rigid set of expectations.

- **Physically move.** Connecting with your physical body can be a way of helping you stay in the present. It can increase your gratitude surrounding your abilities and connects you to the here and now.

- **Breathe.** Breathe deeply into your stomach. This is the body's natural and most relaxing way of breathing, but it is often thwarted by anxiety and other unconscious thoughts. Breathing deeply into your stomach can help relax your body, lower anxiety, and change your thought pattern from urgent to more mindful. Deep breathing sends the message to your brain that everything is okay, and it can slow down its processes.

SELF-CARE

There are a number of different ways to take care of yourself. One of the most essential is taking care of your primary needs, such as eating enough nutritional food, getting adequate sleep, and maintaining your health in general. Another way of caring for yourself is by nurturing your own emotional being. This is an important part of parenthood and is one that often goes neglected. The better your personal and emotional needs are addressed, the more mindful you will be able to be with your child. Take the time for internal reflection, as doing so will help you understand your thoughts and emotions to provide clarity regarding your current life situation.

Maintaining a balance of self-care while taking care of your family can be tricky. However, this balance is a great way to become more aware of where your conscious attention is going. This can bring you greater overall satisfaction, particularly in regard to your ability to stay in the present moment.

Your child's gender journey is bound to have many twists and turns, and it is important to take care of yourself so that you have the strength and endurance to be whole and happy along this journey. If you are the kind of parent who pours all of your energy and emotion into your children, reconsider this. Taking time for yourself feeds your inner spirit and leaves you more capable of supporting other little beings.

IT'S NOT PERSONAL

So much of parenting feels intensely personal. You create this little being and you are very invested in how they turn out. It can feel so personal that you, the parent, can personalize things that have nothing to do with you. For example, your child's gender is not a personal reflection of you or even something for you to be heavily personally invested in. This may sound silly because all parents are invested in their children. However, gender is a core part of who your child is. It is a part of their being. It is not a reflection of you, nor is it something you can or should try to control.

If you let yourself become too personally enmeshed in the gender of your child, then the exploration of gender or transition of gender may feel like an affront to you. Please know this is a function of your own projection of thoughts and feelings onto your child, and is not an accurate representation of what is actually happening. As your child explores their gender, they are coming to know their authentic self. Their authentic self is separate from your being.

> When a conscious parent is in tune with the fact that their child is a separate being, their child's behaviors and motivations feel less personal.

Additionally, parents can feel as though a child's assigned gender at birth is "status quo" and anything other than that is a disruption. If you feel that your child changing their gender is disrupting something that was once okay just the way it was, then you may not be allowing yourself to connect deeply with your child. Your child is simply letting you know what always was; they are not doing something to upset you or disrupt your idea of how things are. When it starts to feel personal, take the time to soothe and care for those feelings that arise. Don't ignore them. Taking care of yourself will enable you to better care for your child.

Utilize Your Strengths

Given you have chosen to read a book about both gender identity and conscious parenting, chances are you already have a foundation of conscious parenting, or at least the desire to be a conscious parent. This shows intention, and making parenting choices with intention is a core foundation of conscious parenting.

Just as it is important for you to recognize the many gifts your child brings to the table, you should also recognize your many inherent gifts. You have many strengths that you bring to support your child in their gender journey. Being present will allow you to move forward and utilize these strengths while at the same time help you alleviate feelings of self-doubt and anxiety.

When things become complicated or feel overwhelming, it can be hard to identify the successes that are likely occurring every day. Make a list of successes you've had in the past year or detail your own qualities that have made this journey easier. If you are struggling to identify your own strengths, turn to someone you trust to help remind you.

Many different skills and talents can be put to task when supporting a gender-expansive child. You may excel at research, advocacy, creativity, policy change, supporting other parents, or problem-solving. You do not need to be good in all areas. Join with other parents and combine strengths and resources. Coming together can fill in holes and make your journey easier.

Be sure to celebrate your accomplishments. This enhances your self-respect, and can help you value and appreciate yourself. In turn, feeling valued and appreciated can enhance your level of conscious awareness. Valuing and appreciating yourself will help in those moments when you feel slightly discouraged or depleted.

Be Forgiving and Kind to Yourself

Consciousness is a constant state of evolution with no end point. It is not a perfect journey. The key to being a conscious parent while walking with your child on their gender journey is in recognizing when you get off course so you can bring yourself back on track. There will be times when you will be triggered by your own past or your own unmet needs, and those emotions will take you away from the present with your child. Small but important successes include times when you can recenter yourself and reground yourself, so that you can be mindful on the walk with your child.

Just as you show grace to your child, so should you show grace to yourself. Give yourself room to feel your authentic feelings without judgment. Give yourself room for mistakes, and forgive yourself easily when you make them. As long as you are traveling down this path with good intention, you certainly are deserving of forgiveness. Tune into your running dialogue in your head. Is it largely positive or negative? If negative, how can you turn those thoughts into something more neutral or positive? Perhaps you need a reminder of the many successes you've made so far, and the genuine good intentions you have for being a conscious parent and supporting your child.

Most conscious parents wouldn't berate or belittle their child for making a mistake. Therefore, it's just as important that you don't do that to yourself. Use the same kindness and encouragement you would when responding to a mistake made on behalf of your child.

Support and Assistance

You are never alone. Someone, somewhere is either going through a similar process with their child or has gone through it in the past. Meditating on this idea can help you feel less isolated. As you support and assist your child in their gender-exploration, you should also have support and assistance. You do not have to walk this journey alone. Get connected with other parents of gender-expansive youth, preferably those who have walked a similar path. Receiving validation and relating to someone who has experienced similar things can be invaluable to you. However, even while you connect with others, stay grounded to yourself and know that no one's experience will be just like yours.

Therapy can be useful as your own source of support and a place where you can be heard fully. Therapy can also help you process feelings associated with your child's gender journey and any changes your child has made. Any difficult feelings that arise from your child's gender expansiveness or transition should not be shared with your child, but rather with someone who is trained to objectively help you process your own emotions. Preferably, you would work with a therapist who has some experience with the gender-affirmative model. This way you are not spending your time educating the therapist or answering questions that could potentially stall your progress.

> In addition to the help therapy can provide in the here and now, it is crucial that you heal your old emotional wounds. Old emotional wounds are what interfere with your ability to consciously parent and may arise when you are trying to be mindful.

Staying Connected to Others

At times, parents of gender-expansive children can find themselves in an interesting predicament. Even as they are encouraging their child to be their authentic selves, the parents themselves may struggle with sharing authentically with others. This can lead to isolation or avoidance of social interactions, even in situations where the parent was previously much more social. The parent may fear a lack of understanding and may therefore choose to avoid social settings rather than answer questions about their child's gender expansiveness. However, just as you would not want your child to isolate themselves in an effort to avoid difficult social situations, neither should you. Being social and surrounding yourself with friends and other parents may be crucial to your well-being. Listen to yourself and your needs, and then respond accordingly. Be confident in your ability to connect with others, assertively address questions, and set boundaries when necessary.

If you have been previously wounded by a friend or loved one's response to your child's gender expansiveness, decide whether or not the relationship is important enough to you to pursue. If it is, have an honest conversation with the person and let them know how their comments or questions hurt you. Let them know what you need as a parent of a gender-expansive child, and then see if they can agree to move forward in a more productive manner. Remember, all relationships involve some type of projection. It is up to you to set boundaries so that you do not become someone else's screen.

Important Points to Consider

It's essential that you take care of yourself while taking care of your gender-expansive child. This includes both your emotional and physical health. Here are some things you need to keep in mind as you travel with your child on their gender journey:

○ Pay close attention to how well you are caring for your own basic needs: sleep, quality of food, and physical movement, to name a few. Making sure these are accounted for will help lay the foundation for your own strength and coping skills.

○ As personal as it may feel, your child's gender is not a personal reflection of you, nor is it tied to your unique being. It is simply a reflection of their unique self.

○ You have many strengths. Utilize these strengths to not only support your gender-expansive child but also yourself. Remind yourself of your many gifts and talents when you are feeling lost.

○ Be kind and forgiving to yourself much as you would your child. You are a human, and along this journey you deserve internalized unconditional love and acceptance.

○ You need not be isolated during this journey, and it is important that you reach out when you need help. Stay connected to others and pursue therapeutic resources when the need presents itself.

Appendix A:
Sample Letter from Parents

Introducing [Name] . . .

Dear Family and Friends:

As a part of our family's "village," we wanted to share some important news. After careful deliberation over an extended time, with the assistance of professional counselors, and with unconditional love—but most of all after listening to our child—we have come to realize that the daughter we knew as [Former Name] is really our son [Name].

Is this too soon? This is not a decision any of us has taken lightly, nor is it one made in haste. Looking back, [Name] has exhibited signs of a male gender identity for many years—in fact, as early as three. [Include examples here.]

There was a time during [state which grade] Grade that saw a reversion to a more traditional female gender identity, including a desire to model the outward signs of "girl," like dresses and long hair. Unfortunately, that period was also marked with significant and growing issues of frustration, lack of self-esteem, and increasing physical aggression that were hard to explain, even under the most expansive theories. And, all the while, those episodes were intensifying, not diminishing.

Over the summer of 2014, [Name] first articulated that he felt like a boy . . . not that he simply wanted to dress like a boy or play sports like a boy, but that he really was a boy on the inside. He gradually cut his hair shorter, stopped wearing anything "girl," increased his identification with anything "boy," and began responding to "he" pronouns.

After those conversations and because of our continued inability to manage his emotional well-being, we sought professional counseling, first from a family therapist and later from a leading professional in the field of preadolescent gender identity issues.

Through that process we have seen—and [Name] has expressed clearly through words and actions, and with a characteristic tenacity —that he has the brain and heart of a boy. In addition to being persistent and consistent about his male gender identity, this summer he also became increasingly insistent. As a result, he has chosen to align the outside that people see with the inside that he has always felt. He will be starting the new school year with a new gender identity and a new name of his choosing.

Is this too young? The American Academy of Pediatrics states that most children have a stable sense of their gender identity by age four, and most research confirms that concepts of gender identity are innate and clear from a very early age. There is no evidence to suggest that environmental factors contribute to gender nonconformity. For most of us who have never questioned our gender identity, we can't ever remember a time when we weren't that gender. But what happens if your birth gender doesn't match your "inside" gender? Often, that dissonance isn't recognized until later in life due to a combination of societal expectations, lack of awareness, and fear . . . often with disastrous results.

We believe this is an ideal time for [Name] to transition. He has the luxury of friends and family who will love and support him, he has the luxury of an inclusive school community that values each unique student, and he has the luxury of time before the onset of puberty.

If you choose to talk to your children about this, most guidance suggests a relatively simple explanation: "Some people are born with the brain and heart of a boy, but the body of a girl, and that makes them sad. Sometimes, they want to change the way people see them on the outside, change their name, and have people say 'he' and 'him.' When their friends use the name and words they want, they feel happy." This information is also included in the enclosure.

Is this unusual? Sure. Is it scary? At times. Do we believe we are doing the right thing for our child? Absolutely. Even making this decision with all the love in our hearts, we still have moments of doubt. But what we do know is that every step of this journey has brought our child more happiness, more confidence, and more peace. We expect his final alignment of outside and inside will only bring more of each.

And we are already seeing it. As we have moved closer to this transition and since we have enacted it, we see and feel a carefree sense of joy in [Name] that has been missing for some time . . . and it is growing daily.

Big brother [Brother] just wants [Name] to be happy. So do we. And we believe that you do as well. We request what we assume you would want in the same situation: that you consider this matter with an open mind and an open heart, that you educate yourselves about the issues, and that you approach us all honestly and with compassion.

We value you in our lives and hope that you will trust our decision and remain close to us. But it is our greatest hope and our deepest desire that you will continue to love, accept, and support our child—our son, [Name]—just as you always have.

With profound gratitude,

[Parents]

Appendix B:
Facets and Multiplicities of You

Facets of YOU

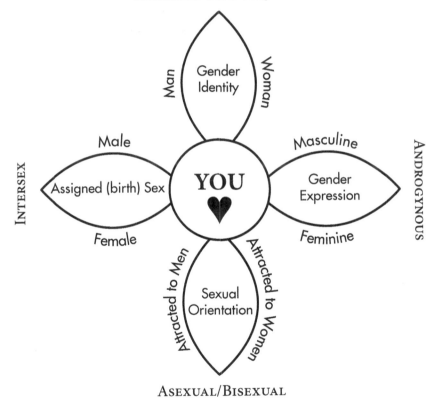

AGENDER/GENDERQUEER

Man — Gender Identity — Woman

Male — Masculine

INTERSEX — Assigned (birth) Sex — YOU 🖤 — Gender Expression — ANDROGYNOUS

Female — Feminine

Attracted to Men — Sexual Orientation — Attracted to Women

ASEXUAL/BISEXUAL

Created by Darlene Tando, LCSW, 2016

Multiplicities of YOU

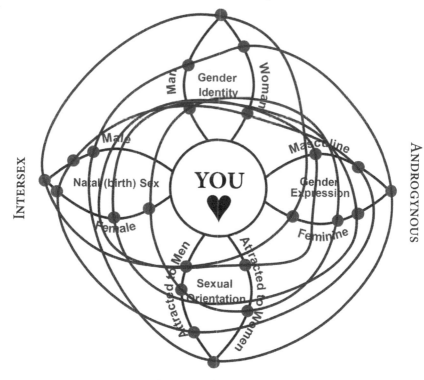

AGENDER/GENDERQUEER

INTERSEX

ANDROGYNOUS

ASEXUAL/BISEXUAL

Man

Woman

Gender Identity

Male

Masculine

Natal (birth) Sex

YOU

Gender Expression

Female

Feminine

Attracted to Men

Attracted to Women

Sexual Orientation

Created by Darlene Tando, LCSW, 2016

Appendix C: Spectrums

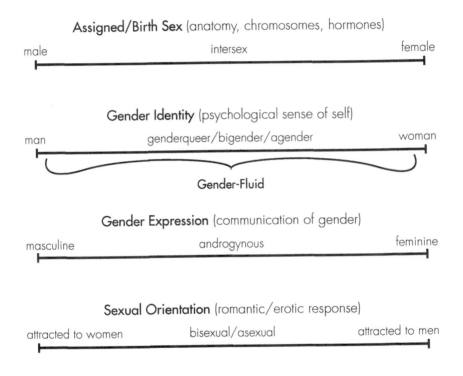

Assigned/Birth Sex (anatomy, chromosomes, hormones)

male   intersex   female

Gender Identity (psychological sense of self)

man   genderqueer/bigender/agender   woman

Gender-Fluid

Gender Expression (communication of gender)

masculine   androgynous   feminine

Sexual Orientation (romantic/erotic response)

attracted to women   bisexual/asexual   attracted to men

Adapted from "Diagram of Sex and Gender" by Center for Gender Sanity, 2009
Modified by Darlene Tando, LCSW, 2016

Appendix D: Transition Worksheet

<u>I KNOW SOMEONE WHO IS CHANGING</u>

My _____ is changing.
(friend, brother, aunt)

They were born a _____ but are changing into a _____.
(boy/girl)   (boy/girl)

Right now I call this person _____.
(old name)

Soon I will be calling them _____.
(new name)

When I talk about them, I will be saying _____ instead of
(he/she)

_____ and _____ instead of _____.
(he/she)   (him/her)   (him/her)

This change will now make this person my _____.
(friend, sister, uncle)

I think it will be _____ for me to use the new name and words for them.
(hard/easy)

I think they will be _____ when I use their new name.
(any feeling)

I feel _____ about this change.
(any feeling)

People I can talk to and ask questions about this change are:

Created by Darlene Tando, LCSW, 2016
www.DarleneTando.com

Appendix E: Resources

Education-Related Resources
National Center for Transgender Equality
www.transequality.org/know-your-rights/schools

Safe Schools Coalition
http://safeschoolscoalition.org

Gender Spectrum
www.genderspectrum.org

"Schools in Transition: A Guide for Supporting Transgender Students in K–12 Schools"
https://www.genderspectrum.org/staging/wp-content/uploads/2015/08/Schools-in-Transition-2015.pdf

GSA Network (Gay-Straight Alliance Network)
https://gsanetwork.org

Gay, Lesbian & Straight Education Network (GLSEN)
www.glsen.org

Welcoming Schools
www.welcomingschools.org

Legal Resources
Transgender Law Center
http://transgenderlawcenter.org

National Center for Lesbian Rights (NCLR)
www.nclrights.org/our-work/transgender-law/transgender-youth

Lambda Legal
www.lambdalegal.org/help

U.S. Department of Education, Office for Civil Rights
http://www2.ed.gov/about/offices/list/ocr/index.html

Family Support Resources
TransFamily Support Services
http://transfamilysos.org/Home.html

TransYouth Family Allies
www.imatyfa.org

Gender Odyssey
www.genderodyssey.org

Parents, Families and Friends of Lesbians and Gays (PFLAG)
http://community.pflag.org/transgender

Bullying and Discrimination Resources
Claim Your Rights resources from PFLAG and GLSEN
http://community.pflag.org/claimyourrights

Lambda Legal "Know Your Rights"
www.lambdalegal.org/know your-rights/how-the-law-protects-lgbtq-youth-0

American Civil Liberties Union
www.aclu.org/issues/lgbt-rights/lgbt-youth/harassment-and-bullying

Know Your Rights: Transgender People and the Law
https://www.aclu.org/know-your-rights/transgender-people-and-law

Miscellaneous Resources
Gender Blog written by Darlene Tando, LCSW
www.DarleneTandoGenderBlog.com

"ID Please!: A Guide to Changing California & Federal Identity Documents to Match Your Gender Identity"
http://transgenderlawcenter.org/issues/id/id-please

The Trevor Project
www.thetrevorproject.org

Appendix F: Classroom Rules

In Our Classroom . . .

We are kind to each other.

All toys are for all children.

Colors are for everyone.

Everyone gets to pick their own style.

Being different is Okay.

We stand up for others.

Created by Darlene Tando, LCSW, 2016
www.DarleneTando.com

Index

Therapists, 93, 131–35
Tightrope visualization, 54, 62–64, 68
Transgender child
    advocating for, 127–28, 194–96, 204
    affirmation of, 99–100, 126
    bullying issues, 182–85, 191–92
    changing mind, 107–9
    changing name, 99–100, 137–38,
        202–3
    coaching, 83, 185–88
    conscious awareness of, 90–91
    consistent traits in, 88–90
    distress of, 89–90, 126–31
    empowering, 187–88, 192
    equipping, 187–92
    explanation of, 85–87
    gender identity and, 86–91
    "hearts and brains" of, 27–28, 92–93,
        100, 172–73
    needs of, 53–54, 72–73, 98
    parenting, 85–100
    persistent traits in, 88–90
    recognizing, 88–91

    support for, 181–92
    teasing issues, 181–92
    temperament of, 88–90, 100
    transitions, 36–37, 96–99, 137–53,
        158–62, 166, 170–74
    trusting, 105–11
    understanding, 26–28
Transition options, 137–48
Transition worksheet, 231
Trouble, borrowing, 119
Trusting self, 101–11
Truth, understanding, 156–60

Validation, 19, 22
Visualization techniques, 103–4, 109,
    111, 146–47, 175

Well-being of child, 15–19
Worries, handling, 103, 109–11, 114–15,
    119–23